BAMBOO WOMEN

Stories from Ming Quong, a
Chinese Orphanage in California

Nona Mock Wyman

For,
Linda

CHINA BOOKS
San Francisco

Radiant Light
Nona

Published in the United States of America by
Sinomedia International Group
China Books
360 Swift Ave., Suite 48
South San Francisco, CA 94080
www.chinabooks.com

Cover design: Nathan Grover
Text design: Linda Ronan

Printed in the United States of America

ISBN 978-0-8351-0006-9

10 9 8 7 6 5 4 3 2 1

Library of Congress Cataloging-in-Publication Data

Wyman, Nona Mock.
Bamboo women : stories from the women of Ming Quong, a Chinese or-phanage in California / by Nona Mock Wyman. — 1st ed.
p. cm.
ISBN 978-0-8351-0006-9 (pbk.)
1.Ming Quong Home (Oakland, Calif.)—History. 2.Ming Quong Home (Los Gatos, Calif.)—History. 3.Chinese-American women—California—History. 4.Orphans—California—History.I. Title.

HV995.O32M558 2012
362.73'2—dc23

2011045298

CONTENTS

ACKNOWLEDGEMENTS

With a heart full of gratitude, I thank all these wonderful people who, each in his or her own special way, helped me with this book.

The Diablo Writer's Workshop in Walnut Creek, California, with Anastasia Hobbet, Jerry Ball, Cinda McKinnon, and Harrietta Heibel.

My editor, Linda Foust.

Jane Stone, Karin Evans, William Wong, Ben Fong Torres, Roy Chan, Jim Wyman, Kevin Welch, Tanya Lonac, Katrina Gee, Kammy Rose, Doris Yee, Kashina Warren, Shawn Jiminez, Susan, PJ, Bethan Lamb, Alex Lock, Lani Owyoung, Paul and Darlene Lee, Pamela Wong, Bob McClean, Carol Lutz, Lissa Hallbergh, Vera Zaskevich, Mauvre Quilter, Dean James, Barbara Wagner, Marlene and Walt Hoy, Lee Anne Quisenberry, Brenda Wong Aoki, Bob Joe, Erica Hatfield, Susan Irene Troop, Monk Khuong Viet McCarthy, and others who read the manuscript or inspired or assisted me in writing this book.

My Ming Quong store customers.

My Ming Quong Home family and Loretta Schauer, the first MQ girl to encourage me to write this book and send it to her!

And now to you, my readers, my deepest appreciation for your interest.

DEDICATION

This book is dedicated to all the Ming Quong women and to all women who have overcome adversity.

"Ming Quong," the Chinese girls' orphanage, means "radiant light" in Cantonese, which is the spiritual interpretation. In the academic sense, it can also translate to "brilliant, bright, and shiny." The two Homes where I grew up were located in Oakland and Los Gatos, on the San Francisco peninsula.

My fascination with bamboo stems from early childhood days at the Home in Los Gatos, where a small stand of wild bamboo grew and survived without care from anyone. We all had jobs at the Home; as a preschooler, mine was helping the nursery teacher with the daily wash. One very cold morning, I noticed a strange sight—white smoke wafting in the air from the hillside below. Perplexed, I finally realized it was the dirty laundry water gushing from an exposed pipe and draining into the bamboo. Surprised, I wondered if the hot suds and bleach would kill the plants. Decades later, while visiting the Home, I was happy to see that the bamboo was not only still there but had grown into a large grove! Later, at my Ming Quong gift store in Walnut Creek, I chatted with a Chinese couple, Marlene and Walt Hoy, telling them how much I loved bamboo, and Marlene remarked that bamboo represents strength and durability. In that moment, I felt a rush of excitement as I realized what bamboo means to me—"the women of Ming Quong!" From that day forth, whenever I have a book reading, I always include the old metaphor, "A good woman is like bamboo; when the winds blow, it bends; it doesn't break."

I especially thank all the women whose stories are told in this book. They had the courage to open up decades of buried childhood secrets. It was sometimes painful to relive the past, and I felt great empathy for all of them. Many of the stories came from life-long friends who had never told me of the suffering they endured as youngsters. Throughout the unfolding of these stories, a sense of incredible strength came through, revealing the remarkable spirit they all possessed—the power of overcoming adversity. Their willingness to reveal their backgrounds completes the human, personal side of the history of Ming Quong that I began in my first book, *Chopstick Childhood in a Town of Silver Spoons*. To all the women of Ming Quong, I sincerely dedicate this book to you. You are all truly the radiant lights of Ming Quong.

INTRODUCTION

In 1935, when I was 2¹/₂ years old, my world shattered. My immigrant mother took me to an orphanage 30 miles away from our home in San Francisco, placed me on a stranger's lap, and walked out the door. I remember screaming in terror as she disappeared from view, but a group of young girls instantly clustered around me and a small hand reached out for mine. I looked up and saw another little girl not much older than I, her eyes were brimming with tears—and I was comforted.

I never saw my mother again.

I grew up there at the Ming Quong Home in Los Gatos, California along with 35 other Chinese girls who became my family, as close as any "true sisters" could be. We were raised by 5 missionary women (3 Caucasian and 2 Chinese who cared for us in their strict manner).

As an adult in my fifties, I began to hear disturbing statements about the Home. One was that "bad" girls lived at Ming Quong and that Chinese parents would threaten to send their daughters there if they didn't behave! Two college students I knew also gave me some startling facts: classroom discussions and a required textbook featuring Ming Quong stated that prostitutes lived at the Home! I was shocked. I couldn't believe these untruths! Never in my thirteen years at the Home had I heard such allegations or seen anything to support them!

A decade later I researched the history of Ming Quong for my first book, *Chopstick Childhood in a Town of Silver Spoons*. As with a puzzle, bits and pieces of facts began to fit together, and by the end of my research, I understood the teachers' staunch silence: they had been protecting us!

The history of Ming Quong dates back to 1915, but in actuality it goes back further, to 1848, when a ten-year-old boy was on a stagecoach from Sacramento, looking forward to a romp in the ocean in San Francisco. Even more exciting, this fourth-grader had a secret which he had sworn not to tell to anyone. However, he heard enthusiastic fellow passengers talking about the rumor of gold having been discovered at the creek at Sutter's Mill, near where he lived. The boy was stunned, as that was his secret! Unable to contain himself, he suddenly burst out, "It's true! Gold was found at Sutter's Mill!" And that's how the whole world came to know of an event that changed American history.

The forty-niner gold rush was on, and in just one year, thousands of fortune-seeking men arrived from all around the world. San Francisco was the main port of entry, and California became a melting pot with a diverse mix of cultures. The Chinese were the first to arrive on "Gold Mountain," as they called it. Newspaper advertisements had encouraged them to make the trip, and they planned to strike it rich quickly and return to China as wealthy, courageous men bringing great honor to their poverty-stricken villages.

Unfortunately, that didn't happen. Discrimination against the Chinese was rampant. The Chinese, with their unusual customs, were too much for the miners to tolerate. American miners ridiculed the long Chinese robes and the single braid which hung down the men's backs. They disliked their food, their speech, and their Eastern philosophy. Caricatures and cartoons depicting the Chinese as heathens showed up around town.

Frontier California was wild, with few laws and even fewer protections for the Chinese people. They essentially had no rights. Although they worked diligently and successfully found gold, it was not theirs to keep! Envious and greedy, American miners jumped their claims and forced the Chinese out of the gold fields. Even worse, many Chinese were murdered. The men had nowhere to turn for help.

During this time of increasing social tension, thousands of Chinese women and young girls came to the United States. Some poverty-stricken families sold their daughters with a promise of a good life in America. Instead, "yellow slavery" was rampant, and Chinese and Caucasian racketeers exploited these young women. Some ended up as domestic drudges, indentured slaves, and prostitutes. A few escaped. Some married merchants, while the legendary Donaldina Cameron of San Francisco's Chinatown rescued others. The latter were fortunate, as these young women had nowhere else to go. They were sheltered and raised at a rescue mission called "920," named after an address on San Francisco's Sacramento Street. There, Caucasian missionary women of the Presbyterian faith—along with a few Chinese women—cared for them. When the mission became too crowded, Cameron separated the young, innocent, orphaned girls from the exploited young women, and the Oakland and Los Gatos Ming Quong Homes opened to house the the children. The latter remained at 920, later known as Cameron House. This history shows how the misinterpretations must have started!

I hope that historians and college professors will point out the errors in the textbooks and that any future class discussions about the Ming Quong Home will be accurate.

Donaldina Cameron was well known for her daring escapades in rescuing Chinese girls, even while endangering her own life. Her fame brought Hollywood knocking at her door with a substantial offer of money for a movie about the girls. She agreed, as the money would be beneficial for the girls' future. After only a few camera shots in the mission's large dining hall, however, Donaldina Cameron saw that the girls would not be accurately portrayed. She immediately stopped the filming and demanded that everyone leave at once. To this day, no one unknown to Cameron House has ever been able to get permission to do a play or a documentary. One of Donaldina Cameron's philosophies was to protect the girls at any expense! Now I fully understand the reason those dedicated teachers didn't answer our questions about why we came to the Home. For this I am eternally grateful. As young girls, we were much too vulnerable to hear stories of prostitutes and hard lives.

When searching for a site for Ming Quong, Donaldina Cameron insisted the new home be located in an area with plenty of sunshine, as many of the girls were in poor health. With the help of many devoted volunteers and her ever-abiding faith in God, Cameron's prayers were answered. She found the perfect spot across the bay in fog-free Oakland, adjacent to Mills College. Captain Robert Dollar of the Dollar Steamship Line donated this choice lot with fragrant eucalyptus trees, and world-renowned architect Julia Morgan designed an elegant Chinese-style home for it. After completion of the home, Julia Morgan personally gave Ming Quong two Chinese porcelain foo dogs to grace the entrance to the courtyard. While the dogs traditionally symbolized protection, she also knew the children would enjoy "riding" and playing on them.

To observe this architectural beauty today, with its lush surroundings, one would never believe that orphans lived there. The girls were always appreciative of their new home, and each year some of them visited Captain Dollar on his birthday, presented him with a bouquet of flowers, and sang the "Happy Birthday" song.

The girls enjoyed the Home near Mills for ten years, but the teachers eventually concluded the girls were growing up and needed to be closer to Oakland's Chinatown and the Chinese Presbyterian Church. They thought the girls should intermingle with the Chinese population to better understand their own culture. Meanwhile,

Mills College, which needed to expand, agreed to trade the Home for a corner site near Lake Merritt and Chinatown in Oakland and a large, fifty-year-old summer home in the foothills of Los Gatos on the San Francisco peninsula. The original Mills Home is now the Julia Morgan School, a middle school for girls.

This Los Gatos summer house became the second Ming Quong Home. It opened in 1935 for the younger girls, ages five to around thirteen years. The Spreckels family, who had made their fortune in the sugar trade, had lost this home during the Great Depression. The two-story house sat on a knoll surrounded by four-and-a-half acres of land. The main building housed the two youngest groups of girls, known as the Nursery and the Starlights. Their sleeping quarters were upstairs in an unheated, screened-off porch, which was very cold in winter. The third group of girls, the Lok Hins (Joy-Givers), were housed above a large, remodelled barn. The last group, the oldest "Cottage" girls, lived in a small wooden cottage with no heat or hot running water.

This second home was a stark contrast to the elegance of the first Oakland Ming Quong. However, the abundance of land for thirty-five or forty girls to explore, the dozens of flower beds, and the variety of wonderful trees, made this the ideal area for the Ming Quong family. Everyone enjoyed the quiet countryside, the endless blue skies, and the warmth of the sun.

The third Ming Quong Home opened on Oakland's Ninth Street in 1936 to house the older girls during their teens. This new, two-story home was reminiscent of Julia Morgan's first Ming Quong design, and her treasured foo dogs once again guarded the girls. Both the Los Gatos and the second Oakland Home operated at the same time. I lived first in Los Gatos and then moved to Oakland when I became a teenager.

The Chung Mei Home was a similar home for Chinese boys located in the small city of El Cerrito, across the Bay from San Francisco. Donaldina Cameron elicited the help of a good friend, Dr. Charles R. Shepard, a Baptist missionary with four years of service in China, to operate the home. Shepherd helped raise eight hundred boys from 1935 to 1954. My brother and four cousins lived there.

We all attended the public schools, as well as one hour of Chinese school each weekday, which was taught at the Home. In Chinese class, we memorized Bible verses, Christmas carols, and the Lord's Prayer in Chinese. We learned to write and pronounce our Chinese names and learned characters from a beginners' reader. We sang China's best known songs of the time, including the rousing "Arise" and the Chinese national anthem.

A classmate at the Los Gatos Elementary School, which we attended while living at the Ming Quong Home, thought we were rich girls bought over from China in order to protect us from World War II! Another Chinese girl, who lived near the Oakland Home, was actually envious of us living in such a big, lovely house!

Ming Quong charged fifty dollars a month with a sliding scale for what a relative could afford. Any unpaid balance was subsidized by the Presbyterian Board of National Missions. Some girls came in with no means of support from any relative, and they were paid for by the city, county, or state, depending on each girl's situation. The long-term teachers, who usually numbered about five per Home, received twenty dollars a month, plus room and board and one day off every week.

Many changes occurred at Ming Quong over the years. This once all-girls home run by single women later admitted Chinese boys and, eventually, accepted children of all nationalities. Personnel changed. The new director of the Los Gatos Home was a married man who lived with his wife and three children in their own separate home on the premises. Other men also joined the staff. Two modern cottages were built for the older children, nestled among the many gardens. The Ninth Street Ming Quong closed its doors in 1958. The Los Gatos Home is still in operation for the care of troubled children of any race or gender.

To some people, the Ming Quong Home was known as an orphanage, but it was never an adoption agency. We never thought of ourselves as orphans. We were simply the girls from the Home. Once some visitors mentioned adoption, and the younger girls huddled together in fear, as they didn't want to be separated from their friends. After that there was no more talk of adoption.

Over the years, I have become more attuned to the problems the teachers faced raising us. I think they were concerned that we would give the appearance of being from a wealthy private school. We lived in a grandiose home, the most beautiful in the neighborhood. One time, we girls rummaged through some boxes in the storage room and found white middy blouses with sailor collars. I loved them immediately. Because of my enthusiasm, the girls designated me to ask Miss Higgins, Head of the Home, if we could wear them. The blouses surprised her, and she asked where we had found them. She thought it over, but to our disappointment, the answer was no, with no explanation. Had we worn those blouses, we would probably have been singled out as "the girls from Ming Quong," contrary to the objective of having us blend in with the other girls in the public school, which we usually did. An article in a Presbyterian brochure pictured us as high-schoolers in a photo captioned, "The Ming Quong Home girls from the Oakland orphanage look just like today's typical girls." We wore "all-American" attire of white blouses, plaid skirts, and saddle shoes.

Once, someone donated a quantity of little red coats to the Los Gatos Home. Every Sunday, we walked down the street to and from church, passing the traffic making its way through town to Santa Cruz, a popular weekend get-away. A sea of uniform red coats, we were a battalion of Chinese girls with shiny black hair (in the traditional rice-bowl style) marching along, unaware of the stares from cars. To cross the street, an older girl quickly grabbed the hands of two younger ones, and the rest of us scampered behind. Relieved, the little girls cried out thank-yous, and the drivers responded with smiles and waves.

The girls called Ming Quong "MQ" or simply "the Home," and it was, in every sense, our home. It provided the family stability we needed, and I have kept in contact with many of the MQ girls. This book, *Bamboo Women*, is a natural sequel to my first book, *Chopstick Childhood*, which began the chronicle of my life growing up at Ming Quong and mentioned some of those who lived there with me. Years later I interviewed other Ming Quong girls about how they came to the Home, what life was like in a Chinese girls' orphanage, and what became of them afterwards. One would think reuniting with childhood friends from the Home would be joyful, and it was. But I was also deeply shocked to learn truths I hadn't known back then—horrifying, unthinkable scenarios that occurred before some of the girls took shelter at Ming Quong. We were all, indeed, fortunate that Ming Quong found us.

What if the Ming Quong Home had not existed? What would have happened to us?

I cannot fathom such a scary scenario, and yet that question is always on my mind: what would have happened to the child slaves, the undernourished children, or the children left alone? We all entered Ming Quong as frightened, confused children lost in a world of disturbing circumstances. Many cried, some clung to their loved ones, while others came in quiet acceptance. We arrived not knowing what lay ahead for us in our new home.

At book readings for *Chopstick Childhood*, someone always asks the "what-if" question. I experience an involuntary shudder and reply, "I don't even want to think about it."

All I know is that I am thankful Ming Quong *was*

there for me. The Home was pivotal in the lives of the girls who lived there. It gave us stability and provided inner strength and a nurturing, safe, dependable environment. The true, life-affirming stories in this book can be read by anyone. I find myself strengthened, again and again, despite the sorrow and tears.

Ready for church on Easter Sunday. Front row (left to right): Rhoda Quan, Bessie Wong, Estelle Jung; Second row (left to right): Nancy Yuen, Lois Woo, Anna Mae Wong. Ruby.

Carol Lum (Masters) with Foo Dog outside the Oakland home.

Los Gatos Nursery Group (left to right): Emmy Diaz, Dolly Tom (Jang), Corrine Louie (Otsuki), Lynda Tong (Yee), Joanne Wong, Sylvia Lew, (unknown girl in black coat).

In front of the Oakland home. Left to right: Leila Young, Nona Mock, Bernice Lee.

Miss Higgins (head of the Oakland and Los Gatos homes) with older girls at the Oakland home. Mrs. Chan, one of the Chinese teachers, is in the middle of the back row just to the right of Miss Higgins.

Dolly Tom (Jang) and Nona Mock on Edna's prized bike at the Los Gatos home.

Dressing up for an impromptu play at the Los
Gatos home. Dorothy Lee, Harlan Sue, Lena
Lee, Louise Chin, Laura Gok, Shirley Louie.

Nursery and Starlight Group under the entrance sign to the Los Gatos home.

The Los Gatos home (former Spreckels estate).

Jenny Lee outside Oakland High School.

Nona Mock (in same outfit as Jenny Lee) in front of the Oakland home (the Foo dogs were a gift from architect Julia Morgan).

LIFE'S TEARDROPS: HOW WE CAME TO MING QUONG

raw—agonizing
greater than a thousand tears
childhood shattering

All during my childhood at the Ming Quong Home and even as an adult, I wondered how we all came to be living at MQ. I knew it was the result of some tragedy in each girl's life, but what was it?"

During a renovation of the Los Gatos Home, workers discovered a historical "ledger of entry" of Ming Quong dating back to 1915. We were astounded and elated, for now, decades later, we could finally find out the reasons we had been sent there. Eastfield Ming Quong Children and Family Services hosted a Ming Quong reunion in Los Gatos and presented each attendee with a copy of the over-sized ledger, with pages and pages of names. We are eternally grateful to Eastfield Ming Quong (Ming Quong merged with Eastfield, another orphanage in San Jose) for giving us this pertinent piece of our past.

Now, finally, I would know what my "emergency" had been. Eagerly looking under the column marked, "Reason for Entry," I read, "unfit home" and "health of child." That was all. No mention of the emergency. I was so disappointed.

"Unfit home" was so vague; it sounded as if I had come from a terrible environment. Although I had been very young when I came to the Home—just under three—I had memories of my time before then, and they were not bad ones. Perplexed, I wondered what "unfit home" really meant. Nor was I sick when I arrived at the Home, although seven months later I was rushed to the county hospital with TB. So what did this "health of child" truly mean? Then I understood! The teachers' code of silence about our pasts was also in effect in the ledger! The original administrator, Donaldina Cameron, insisted the teachers not tell us about our origins in order to "protect the children." The past was the past, and it should stay there. Our "secrets" were intact after all these years.

As a child, I accepted this silence, but one girl in particular did not. Younger than me, she lived at the Home after I left. Constantly outspoken, she insisted that the teachers tell her why she was there. She never received an answer, and to this day, she is full of bitterness.

The most frequently asked question of a former Ming Quong girl is, why did you go to Ming Quong? The question is answered below for some. The teachers would have been surprised and even disturbed to know that many of the young girls actually knew the facts. Some found out the reason later in life. Here is a sampling:

Bernice Lee (Goo) and her brother were running wild around San Francisco Chinatown with no supervision while their father worked as a waiter. They were seven and nine years old. Bernice came to Ming Quong, and her brother went to the Chung Mei Home for boys in El Cerrito.

The mother of Louise Chin (Won) had TB. Her father owned a gambling house in San Francisco Chinatown.

The sister of a Ming Quong girl volunteered this story after she had read *Chopstick Childhood*: "My parents had an argument. My father's ultimatum to my mother was, 'Pick between me and your daughter.' My mother picked my father, so that's how my sister (the oldest of what was eventually five siblings) came to the Home."

Sylvia Lew arrived at Ming Quong as the result of her parents' bitter divorce.

After the mother of Emmy Diaz (Brown) died, her father took her to the Home to get her away from her aunt, who wanted to take her to China. Emmy was traumatized at being torn away from her aunt's embrace and didn't see her father again for two years, as he was a successful businessman working in Panama.

The younger of two sisters who wish to remain anonymous shared, "I saw my dad chase my mom around the bed, and when he caught her, he tried to strangle her with a towel, which I tried to pull away. Our mom died when Dad stabbed her with a knife."

As related by her sister, Dorothy Lum, Virginia Chung was supposed to enter into an arranged marriage, as was the Chinese custom. She was fourteen, and the man was twenty. By American law, she was too young to marry, so she was placed at Ming Quong until she was sixteen.

Another girl had a Chinese father and a Caucasian mother. Her father was murdered by a racist. When her mother died, she came to the Home, which by then had begun accepting mixed-race children.

Lillian Fong (Lew) had a bout with tuberculosis at age eleven and needed a healthy, sunny climate in which to recover. Los Gatos was chosen, as it was reportedly the second best area for recovery, next to Egypt.

Six-year-old Marie Yeong (Ranta) was an abused child. Her mother, a severely disturbed individual, took her wrath out on Marie.

Bessie Wong (Aoki) came to the Home next to Mills due to socio-economic differences. Her father was a seaweed gatherer, while her Eurasian mother, used to a life of wealth and servants, came from Australia. After the birth of her fourth child, Bessie's mother decided to leave her life with her husband, gathered up her children, and literally ran away. The oldest sister stayed with the mother, and Bessie came to Ming Quong, while her two brothers went to Chung Mei.

And now my story at the Oakland Home begins, followed by stories about other Ming Quong girls. The stories came from interviews and include my insights about each situation, thus adding another dimension to what we all experienced at the Home.

NONA AT THE OAKLAND HOME

once again—it's me
thought my first book was enough
but readers said, "No!"

The most frequent question people ask after reading my first book, *Chopstick Childhood*, is, "What happened to you after you left the Los Gatos Home and moved to the Oakland Home?"

In truth, it was one cultural shock after another. From a serene countryside with no close neighbors, I moved to a noisy city with neighbors just a few feet away. In Oakland, there was chaotic traffic at every intersection; one had to be careful of fast cars screeching around the corners.

The schools were vastly different in appearance: from a Spanish-style, two-story hacienda structure to a nondescript, two-story, brick building that resembled a formidable institution. Chinese students were always a minority in Los Gatos, but on the first day of school at Oakland's Lincoln Elementary, the majority of kids on the crowded, concrete playground were Chinese.

A rude awakening to me was the crude actions of some Caucasians students who were so completely different from the well-mannered classmates I was accustomed to. Once I was bent over at the water fountain, when a loud-mouthed girl from my class waltzed by and flipped up my dress. Stunned and embarrassed, with a mouthful of water, I did nothing but endure the raucous laughter of her friends behind my back.

At that time I was thirteen, a gangly individual with a trusting nature. Sitting in front of me in the classroom was a guy who was quite small for his age. His appearance was slovenly. He wore the same striped tee-shirt every day and had dirty fingernails. His hair was matted with grease, and his glasses were the thickest I had ever seen. All that would have been fine if he had kept to himself. But he didn't—he violated me physically! This uncouth guy put his hand down behind his desk and ran his fingers up and down my leg. I scooted over as far as possible, but he still managed to reach me! I was stymied! Of course I was too mortified to tell the classroom teacher or the teachers at the Home. To this day I always wonder if anyone saw what transpired. His last name was Silva, but I nicknamed him Saliva—it helped a little to give him a repulsive name. No one knew about Saliva until just recently, when I was reminiscing with another former Lincoln School student.

Such bad memories! As I write this, I half-heartedly chuckle at the nickname and wonder why I'm dredging this up now. But, like the other Ming Quong women who share their stories and experiences in this book, I know that our lives were different being raised in an all-Chinese girls orphanage in America. The telling of our stories can only bring more understanding to everyone in all walks of life and perhaps help another child who feels alone in a similar predicament. In other words, don't be afraid or embarrassed; don't just keep it inside: tell someone!

At the Oakland Ming Quong, the first roommate the teachers gave me was the prettiest, shapeliest girl at the Home. She was four or five years older than me. I knew her from the Los Gatos Home. She had lived at the Oakland Home once before, but because she was "boy crazy," she had been sent back down to live at the Los Gatos Home for a time. She sobbed loudly and hysterically at being there, and I wondered how a boy could make her so unhappy and how she could hate the same

Home that I loved! Her last name was Woo. Once she gave me a glamorous picture of herself, and I titled it, "Mary Woo Woo!" Now she was back in Oakland.

Even though I was with other girls I grew up with in Los Gatos, I missed the Los Gatos Home itself, which had been comforting. The Oakland MQ was too confusing, and there was too much going on.

I couldn't sleep my first night in Oakland. The back of the Home was located on a busy corner, and we had to keep our second-floor bedroom windows open for fresh air. Loud traffic and blinking signal lights left me tossing and turning all night. It made me all the more homesick. Gone were the serene nights in Los Gatos. I missed the star-spangled skies and just lying quietly in bed listening to a lone owl hooting.

Mary Woo Woo, who was still up rolling her long, thick hair in curlers, said, "What's the matter? Can't you sleep? I love it here. In fact, I can't sleep *unless* it's noisy!"

My thoughts were, "Geez, she's mean and hard!

Yet she did have one comforting thought: "Don't worry; you'll get used to it!" She was right. Eventually I was able to tune out the noise and fall asleep instantly. Slowly I adjusted to the hectic city life.

Later we were able to pick our own roommates with approval from the teacher in charge. One of my roommates was Lucianne (name changed). Lucianne was an-other attractive, outgoing girl with brownish hair. I think she was Eurasian. We became good friends and called each other "twins" and "sisters." Lucianne was not like my other "twin sister," Jenny. Lucianne and I looked nothing alike. I was skinny, while she had a full figure. She was a leader and became president of the girls at the Home. Even though the girls had voted for me to be president, I had declined; not wanting to talk to Miss Higgins, the head of the Home, about any grievances we girls might have. Instead, I became vice president. We also voted for a secretary, who took the minutes, and a treasurer. Why the club-like atmosphere? I never knew. The teachers probably wanted us to live in a democratic-type of envi-ronment in hope that we would become good, responsi-ble people. Or perhaps it was because Miss Higgins had graduated from Vassar, a private college where clubs were prominent.

Lucianne triggered the scariest experience I'd ever encountered at the Home. One time in the bedroom while talking about boys, she picked a fight with me because she thought I had flirted with her boyfriend. Surprised, I denied it, but she didn't believe me. I re-ally thought she was kidding, but the tension in her face mounted, and I finally realized she was serious. I headed for the open door, but as I reached it, she tried to block my exit. In doing so, she actually shoved me out of the doorway. I skidded down the long hallway, which was the length of a basketball court. Because the wooden floor was well waxed, I slid all the way to the end. Before I really knew what had happened, Lucianne pursued me.

The few girls who heard the commotion were petri- fied and aghast. Trapped in a corner, I was dumbfounded. Gathering my wits about me, I attempted to get up but was too late. Lucianne lunged at me like a wild animal after its prey. What a temper! She was strong as an ox and much bigger than me. I knew I had no chance for surviving this onslaught. But then my instincts kicked in, and with all my might, I grabbed her arms and tried to shove her away from me.

Suddenly she stopped and straightened up, her face startled and hurt. Then she half-laughed and conceded. "Don't ever fight with Nona," she said. "She's got sharp nails." What had happened? What did she mean and why her sudden change of attitude? Then I glimpsed her upper arms; angry red welts had formed where my nails had scratched her.

What a memory! The art of growing up! It sounds bad, and it was. It was a miracle I had survived. The strange thing about that horrifying experience is that we remained friends! Maybe she realized I had told the truth, but who really knows? From what I knew about Lucianne, she had been in many foster homes. Her father had a shady background and was cruel to her and her mother and eventually deserted them. Maybe all these facts caused her hardships and explained her behavior. As for me, I never felt fear from Lucianne again. Ming Quong became a really peaceful place to live. My fighting incident was the only one I ever knew about.

During the Christmas season, we girls participated in the annual play about the birth of Jesus at our local Chinese Presbyterian Church. Miss Musgrave assigned each interested girl a role. I did not want to perform, as I was too self-conscious. I watched as the girls raised their hands for the roles they wanted. The chosen girl grinned with pleasure while the others sighed in disappointment. As always, when the role of the angel came up, all hands shot up for this honor. Miss Musgrave scanned their hopeful faces and then looked at me and stopped. Uh-oh, why did she hesitate? What was she thinking? Then the unexpected happened. She said, "Nona, you will be the angel."

I groaned softly, "But I don't want to be in the play." She paid no attention to my remark. I knew my comment was in vain. I had no choice. I had to do my part.

That was the order of things at Ming Quong. Reluctantly, I memorized my part. Those few lines seemed like the longest Bible verse ever.

When performance day arrived, I donned a white sheet. As the light shone down on me on stage, I suddenly knew what stage fright meant. Trembling slightly, I bravely raised one arm to the startled shepherds on the hillside, who were flabbergasted by the presence of an angel in their midst. I began: "Fear not, for behold, I bring you good tidings of great joy, which shall be to all people. For unto you this day is born in the city of David, a Savior which is Christ, the Lord. And this shall be a sign unto you. Ye shall find the babe wrapped in swaddling clothes lying in a manger."

That was it. What a relief; I had made it. It seems short now, but it seemed to last forever at the time.

Miss Musgrave's insightfulness in assigning me the role planted a seed that helped me overcome something I feared! I am forever grateful.

These two different episodes during my teen years—being a frightened non-fighter and a scared angel—were the beginning of my learning how to stand on my own two feet.

Lucianne nicknamed me "Greenhorn" because I was the most naïve person around! I thought the nickname was funny, and I added "#1" to make it more comical. At least it was better than my other nickname, "Big Head"! I was also called "Big Eyes."

Well, being Greenhorn #1, I was in the dark about what Lucianne and another good friend of ours named Francesca (name changed) were doing in the evenings! When the household was asleep, these two girls slipped out the back door and went out for the evening! Here I was, Lucianne's roommate, and I never ever realized she was gone! If anything, I thought she went down the long hallway to the bathroom and was taking a long time!

The teacher on duty always locked all the doors for the night and left the two girls out in the dark. As it happened, Jean Yee's bedroom was on the first floor, so Lucianne and Francesca would knock on her window to awaken her, and she would let them in! She was so innocent she thought the girls were just out for fresh air. Jean never tattled on the girls. To this day, however, she always keeps two sets of keys to her home with her at all times, for fear of being locked out.

Finally, the teacher caught on. Suddenly Francesca was no longer living at the Home. She had been caught a few blocks away at the Colonial Inn in some man's room! We were aghast. We all knew the man, a nice, older Chinese guy who owned a shrimp business near Oakland Chinatown, located just four blocks from the Home. Shortly thereafter, the Home found Lucianne a house-job with a local family, and she moved out of Ming Quong. She remained a junior in high school, however, and I saw her at Oakland High, so our friendship continued.

Though I was a "greenhorn," I did have a few boyfriends. If you liked a boy, you could bring him to the Home and introduce him to the teachers in hope they would approve of him. If they did, you could go out on an official date! Once I brought home Morris, an "older" guy—in other words, he was out of high school. He was as nice and handsome as could be! How could anyone not like him? He smoked, which I knew the teachers wouldn't approve, so before he came over, he refrained from smoking. I can't even remember if we went out on an official date, but I do remember enjoying a cold Coke with him at a Chinatown soda fountain that happened to be in a corner liquor store. I never noticed the words, "Liquor Store," on the outside of the building! But Miss Higgins called me in and drilled repeatedly about whether I had drunk anything besides Coke! "You didn't drink anything else? Are you sure?" I had no idea what she was getting at! "So why do you go in there?" she asked. I didn't reply, but the answer in my mind was that cute guys hung out there, and what else was there to do? Yes, we window-shopped and played on the playground, but Chinatown was much more intriguing.

When I got to Oakland High, I was assigned to work as a typist for a counselor, Mr. Ketchum, who was also the football coach. He was kind and particularly patient with my slow typing. One day, the star quarterback and a couple of other burly, gregarious players lumbered into the office where I was slowly pecking away on the typewriter keys with my back to the door. I heard them snickering behind my back as they imitated my slow tapping. My face flushed with embarrassment. Then they stopped, and there was complete silence. Mr. Ketchum had said or done something to make them leave me alone. Decades later, a TV program documented the life of a great coach, and it was Mr. Ketchum! It was nice to see. He was indeed a good, kind man to all: an unforgettable man.

Life was fine. I was happy. I had assimilated into my new life. Abandonment brought me to Ming Quong, but I quickly adjusted and made a new life there. I lived at the Oakland Home from age thirteen, after spending about ten years in the Los Gatos Home. Then, at age sixteen, I was abandoned again, this time by the Oakland Home I had come to love. Why? Because at that age, girls had to leave Ming Quong! That part of growing up was never a subject we girls or the teachers ever talked about. It just suddenly happened! And now my time had come.

That morning, all the girls went to school, unaware that I was leaving. There were no good-byes, nothing. Getting in the car with my social worker, Miss Ritsey, I tearfully looked back for the last time at the familiar sights I loved: the grand architecture, the beautiful palm tree, and the proud, glistening foo dogs guarding the entrance to the Oakland Home. We loved those dogs; they were always included in all the pictures we took. My heart, completely broken, cried its fond farewell to all.

As the car rounded the corner, hot tears rained down my flushed face, and I cried all the way to my destination, Palo Alto, which was my birthplace. The Home had found me a live-in house job with an older couple and their grade-school daughter. Miss Ritsey tried her best to comfort me. I never forgot her kindness, but that day remains one of the worst experiences of my life.

Perhaps I could have obtained a different live-in job, in Oakland. I now believe the teachers were trying to protect the Greenhorn by sending me across the Bay, away from my daring friends and the fast-paced urban life.

Some former Ming Quong girls feel the Home did

not prepare us well for the "outside world." There were, for example, hasty youthful marriages by girls who didn't really have any idea of what else to do with their lives. Some girls went into marriages with inappropriate or abusive men, having had little experience with the opposite sex at Ming Quong.

Despite some setbacks, I survived to have a fulfilling life, eventually marrying and having a son, Jim. I own and operate a gift store, "Ming Quong," in Walnut Creek, California. Jim's jewelry and gift business has been added, and it is now two stores in one.

I kept in touch with many of my Ming Quong friends throughout our lives, and I have met others at reunions. Now I share their stories.

3

MUI JAI

baby adopted
not for love, but selfishness
deceiving parents

The phone rang. It was Rhoda Quan (Wing), a former Ming Quong girl. Rhoda, a high-energy person, was my former roommate, along with my sister, Emma, during our single days in Oakland after leaving the Home. The three of us lived in a nicely furnished, two-bedroom apartment on Twenty-Second Street, a half-block from Lake Merritt. We ran our household efficiently, just as the Ming Quong Homes had been run. Each of us had our chores—grocery shopping, cooking, vacuuming, and keeping track of the money allotted for each week's food. And as in the Homes, we rotated our jobs.

Hearing from my good friend was always a pleasure. The day she called, Rhoda was extremely excited about my first book, *Chopstick Childhood*, which had just been published. Tumbling over her words, she heaped joyful accolades my way. Then she suddenly added that her own memories had surfaced.

"Really?" I exclaimed with excitement. "What kind of memories?"

By now, Rhoda's voice was barely audible. With my ear glued to the receiver, I strained to grasp each word. And what she told me caused a prickly sensation throughout my body. For, over sixty-five years later, this recollection, which she had never divulged to any of the MQ girls, was now spilling forth.

"Nona," she gasped, "I was a mui jai!"

There was silence on my end as I grappled with the words. I was just about to speak when she blurted: "Do you know what a mui jai is?"

Before I could answer, she lowered her voice and exclaimed, "I was a slave!"

"A slave!" I hissed back. "You were a slave?"

"Yes, I was a child slave!"

"I remember reading about mui jais in Donaldina Cameron's book. Wow, you were actually a mui jai? I can't believe it!"

Now, here, at last, is Rhoda's incredible story:

When she was a baby, her parents could not afford to

take care of her, so they gave her away to what is known as a "dynasty" family. This large, traditional Chinese family was very prominent and well known in the San Francisco Bay Area. They lived in the Grand Lake area of Oakland.

The matriarch of the family was from China, and she had bound feet, a sign of wealth and great femininity. She could only take "baby steps" and constantly hollered at Rhoda, her mui jai—her slave—to fetch her slippers. If Rhoda didn't get them quickly, she was beaten with a baseball bat. Rhoda's body was completely covered with welts, and at night the pain was unbearable. She and the two other mui jai in the household slept in the basement, so other members of the family could not hear their cries at night.

The mui jai were always hungry, as they could eat only foods left over from the family's meals. The mui jai did all the household chores, and, unlike the children in the matriarch's family, they never received an allowance. So Rhoda and Jackie (name changed), who bonded and called each other "sisters," frequently followed the milkman's route and emptied the tip money from the milk containers. Sometimes they would even climb over fences to retrieve this treasure! Then they were just like the other children in the family; they too had some money of their own!

There was one thing in their horrific life that was truly just like that of the family's children: they always dressed well. To the unsuspecting outside world, everything was just fine, and for a long time, no one knew the truth of their slavery.

However, there was one woman in the household (a second-generation Chinese) who attended the Chinese Presbyterian Church in Oakland and who, as Jackie has said, was a true Christian. This woman knew that the Ming Quong Home would help these two "sisters," so she planned an escape for them. The woman instructed Rhoda, the oldest (she was now ten), how to take the street car and where to get off to arrive at the Ming Quong Home at 51 Ninth Street in Oakland. The woman gave her tokens for the fare and said Miss Higgins, the head of the Home, was expecting them. Rhoda memorized the escape plan, and when the right time arose, she and Jackie ran as fast as they could. They caught the right streetcar and ran all the way to the Home. Miss Higgins opened the front door to their new home. They were now safe.

Once inside, Miss Higgins, who was aware of the girls' physical abuse, quickly checked out their bodies, and what she saw hastened her efforts to get them out of Oakland right away. The two were driven immediately to the safety of the Los Gatos Ming Quong Home.

In an effort to get her mui jais back, the matriarch visited the girls in Los Gatos after hearing where they were at her church. She brought gifts and tried to bribe them into coming back, but they would not even talk to her.

When the other girls her age moved on to the Oakland Home, Rhoda stayed in Los Gatos to help Miss Reber, the cook, in the kitchen. She didn't learn this was the reason she was left behind until she grew up. As an adult, Rhoda became involved in the culinary world through her passion for cooking. She taught Asian cooking at Laney College in Oakland and the University of California, Berkeley, and for many years she volunteered her culinary skills at the local senior center program. She has worked with television personalities such as Martin Yan and the late Shirley Fong Torres. Rhoda's achievements despite her traumatic beginnings are indicative of her "bamboo strength."

Today one of Rhoda's greatest joys is being a "Pau Pau" (grandma) to her adorable granddaughters. Whenever my friend talks about her family, her entire face lights up, and tears begin to form in her happy eyes. I know the reasons for those tears, as my conscientious friend was a single parent for years. She raised her two daughters well. Her first daughter, Lisa, is a production and sourcing manager for Don't You Want to Peek, where her daughters, Dylan and Kaia, are models. Rhoda's other daughter, Cindy, was a forensic scientist and is now a Consumer Safety Officer for the Food and Drug Administration.

The teachers at Ming Quong would be so proud of this little mui jai who braved obstacles all her life and overcame them in a Christian way. She has always given back so much to the community and especially to her friends.

4 MIDDLE SISTER

a sad beginning
yet child-like smile
was always her way

Jackie (name changed) was Rhoda's younger "sister," and her escape from slavery as a mui jai was described in the preceding chapter. Unlike Rhoda, Jackie was a quiet individual with child-like characteristics. She possessed the cutest smile, coupled with an infectious laugh.

Jackie lived at both the Los Gatos and Oakland Homes. To this day, she is grateful and happy that she and her sister ran away from what she termed "the mean old lady who always whipped us with a baseball bat and who never gave us enough to eat." She added, "Without Ming Quong, we wouldn't be here."

After she left Ming Quong in Oakland, Jackie did housework for a living. She met a Chung Mei boy who had a reputation as a playboy, and who had dated quite a few MQ girls. He introduced Jackie to his brother. She went around with them both, but in the end, she married the brother. Her husband was like Jackie—quiet and gentle—and he had an infectious smile similar to Jackie's. They made a cute couple. They had two daughters. Jackie is currently enjoying her grandchildren and working for a McDonald's restaurant.

5

LOST LOVES

reaching out for love
tiny child restrained
scarred inside and out

Carol Lum (Masters), my lifelong friend, was my first pre-school playmate at the Los Gatos Home when I was around four years old. As the two youngest, we stayed home while all the older girls attended school, and we became very close. As teenagers, we moved to the Oakland Home together. Even after we left the Home, we often spent the day together just doing "girl stuff." Later, we double-dated and triple-dated, and I introduced her to her future husband.

Being with Carol transports me back to the spontaneity of carefree days when we said what was on our minds with no thought of hurting anyone's feelings. Talking with her is like being back at the Home, enjoying the frankness of unpretentious friends. Rhoda and Jackie, her older "sisters," were present when I interviewed Carol. These three girls always called each other "sisters," and the rest of us accepted that, although they looked nothing alike.

In her teens, Carol was the epitome of sweetness. Blessed with a wholesome freshness and good looks, she was popular. She was a queen contestant at the annual well-attended Cotton Ball for the Chinese Ladies' Social Club in Oakland. Her date, Jeff, was just as well-liked by all and was the most handsome escort at the affair. Dancing with him, Carol was "candy for the eyes," in her dreamy, organza, polka-dot formal. These two were definitely in "Love Land." That evening, Carol's life was blissful and full of promise for a wonderful future.

That magical night, however, captured only a euphoric moment in her turbulent journey through life. Her existence leading up to meeting Jeff had been a rocky road full of heartbreak and grief.

Carol's mother was the third slave—mui jai—brought over from China to serve the same "dynasty" Chinese family in the East Bay where Rhoda and Jackie were enslaved. When I asked Carol how she got into the household, Carol said in one breath, "Well, I'll tell you. One day the matriarch went shopping, and while she was out, the elder in the family raped my mother, and that's how I was born!"

"Wow," I gasped. "Did the matriarch know what happened?"

Rhoda interjected, "She knew, but no one talked about it."

"And what happened to Carol's mom?" I asked.

"She ran away, but later she came back because she had nowhere else to go."

When Carol arrived at Ming Quong, she was very tiny for her age. Odd, shiny, raised scars marked both her thighs, and when I asked what they were, she responded, "My mother tied me to a chair because she had to go upstairs to do her chores for the family." I asked Carol how she managed to go to the bathroom while strapped to the chair all day. While she couldn't remember, Jackie grimaced and exclaimed, "She was tied to a toilet seat!"

Carol's constant straining against the ropes to be free and join her mother had caused the huge, angry welts on both thighs, which scarred her for life. She was under-nourished and so tiny and scrawny that baby clothes did not fit her. She had to wear doll clothes!

Carol vividly remembers seeing "legs" while tied up—not just a pair of legs, but an army of legs! Because Carol and the three mui jai lived in the basement, her only view was from a window which looked up to the sidewalk. From where she was tied, all she saw and heard were quick, hurried steps. Every morning men's and women's legs walked in one direction. In the evenings, the same legs walked back the opposite way. These legs were going to and from work. That was baby Carol's distraction of the day. No toys, no human contact. Just legs!

Carol was never brought upstairs to the main house, as she was an embarrassment to the elders. The matriarch strictly insisted that she remain hidden from the family at all times.

When Carol was a year and a half old, people from the Alameda County Health Department rang the doorbell, saying that someone had informed them of Carol's situation. They inspected the premises but found nothing! They came back a second time with a search warrant, however, and found Carol tied to her toilet chair.

Carol went first to the Oakland Ming Quong on Ninth Street, as she was too young even for the Los Gatos Home. The older Ming Quong girls helped care for her, and they adored her. They held her constantly. They fed her and fussed over her as though she were a precious little doll. As Carol said, "I was 'queen for a day.'" Many people fell in love with infant Carol in the Home. Offers of adoption were refused because Carol's mother was still in her life, although she never came to visit her.

Every day, Carol and I had fun playing house, swinging on the wooden swings, and simply letting the innocence of childhood dictate our childish antics. Still, Carol longed for her mother. To get our certificates of completion at swimming lessons, each student had to jump off the diving board and swim a few feet to the edge of the pool. We all did—except Carol, who was so scared she couldn't jump. Even when the sympathetic instructor got into the water and assured her he would catch her, she continued to shiver and hug herself in fear. Her reason: "If I jumped, I might die, and I would never see my mother again." Everyone pleaded with her, to no avail. The fear on her tormented face was real, and we were very sad for her.

Each morning Carol and I helped Miss Chew, our Nursery teacher, hang out the wash. We held two wooden clothespins in outstretched hands for her to take quickly instead of having to bend over and fumble for them. She grabbed the pins from each of us in turn. Sometimes she forgot and took from one of us twice in a row, but we never said anything. We just eyed each other and grinned.

After work, when it was one of the gardener's days at the Home, we scampered off to see what he was doing.

Because we were not supposed to bother him or talk to him, we kept our distance. When he dug big holes for new plants, however, we hollered, "Are you going to dig to China?" and he laughed and told us to go off and play. We always minded him and dashed off, happy as larks.

Unbeknownst to me, Carol at age nine became good friends with a boy in her class at the local elementary school. He lived in the only house atop El Sereno Mountain, adjacent to the Home. We could barely see his house, as evergreen trees surrounded it. Once at prayer time, I saw two people slowly climbing the steep mountain. From the picture window in the Home's living room, they looked like ants intent on getting to the top. I loved this mountain and always wondered who lived there. And now over six decades later, I found out. I was in for a shock, and if the teachers had ever found out, who knows what would have happened to Carol!

Carol's friend's parents were always travelling, and he was left on his own much of the time. Carol would sneak out of the Home to visit him. They stayed outside his house just talking. When she told me about this, I gasped, "You went to his house and never got caught?! How did you do it? And is that all you did, just talk?"

Carol replied that she knew the Home's schedule and planned her visits accordingly. As for just talking, she told me they did that most of the time—but they also explored their bodies! Then one day, engrossed in talking, they didn't realize it had become dark. Carol was so frightened that she had the boy walk her down the hill, and she made it back just in time for the last dinner bell!

I couldn't believe that Carol had actually sneaked out two or three times a week and that no one ever knew about her escapades! "I still have his picture," she said.

"Really?" I exclaimed, "What did he look like?"

"Just a regular guy. He was blond."

Carol's mother never came when other parents or relatives visited the other girls in Los Gatos. She knew her mom was still alive, and she felt completely abandoned and painfully alone. She believed no one cared about her. To escape her misery, she would go to an unused water shed and climb the narrow, winding stairs to sit for hours looking out a small, upstairs window. She felt safe there, and no one saw her tears, as we seldom used the small water tower.

Carol is now deaf in one ear and wears a hearing aid. She told us the reason for this was not "old age." The doctor said that her ear drum was ruptured from all the "batting" she received when young. She noticed the shocked expressions of Rhoda, Jackie, and me and firmly repeated, "Yeah, they [the teachers] always batted me around."

Carol's strength and stamina propelled her forward, and her experiences did not leave her bitter; she still has a good sense of humor. Still, her beginnings and her childhood experiences spilled over into her adult life, resulting in some tragic results.

As I mentioned before, she met her husband through me. A really nice guy, he had been interested in me, but I had begun dating my future husband and thought the other man would probably like Carol. He did, and she liked him, so they married and had two great children. It was a good life until her husband's emotional problems and physical abuse terminated their marriage. After that, Carol's life took a drastic spin downwards. Her later involvement with another man resulted in a son, whom she gave up for adoption. With a different man, she had a baby girl, whom she also gave up. The pain was evident in Carol's demeanor as she exposed more of her tumultuous life.

I asked how she felt giving up her babies.

"Very hard," she said, tearing up. "I couldn't even hold them, because if I did, I knew I wouldn't be able to give them up." The fact that she placed her babies for adoption came from her feeling that the children's welfare comes first.

During this period, Carol was a waitress in Bay Area Chinese restaurants, and at different times she also owned three restaurants, one in Oregon with a boyfriend. She took care of her two children as best as she could, but she began drinking too much. She never drank while working, but she constantly eyed the clock. As closing time approached, her throat became dry and parched just thinking of that first drink after work. Every evening she was completely zonked out, and her children would have to undress her and put her to bed. Then it hit her that she was an alcoholic, and she realized what her young children were going through. Just like that, she quit drinking. "That was it," she said, and she's been sober ever since.

Carol crossed paths with her mother again, but not until she was an adult. What she had always wanted more than anything else in her life came true at Rhoda's wedding, where Jackie and members of the "dynasty" family that had enslaved them were in attendance. It may seem inconceivable that the former mui jais gathered together with the dynasty family, but the children of that family were nice and not at all like their cold-hearted elders.

Someone at the wedding pointed out a tiny but sturdily built woman to Carol and said, "That is your mother." Carol did not approach her then, but after the wedding they all went to Rhoda's apartment, where Carol and her mother sat a short distance from one another. They kept staring at each other, as if transfixed. Finally, Carol couldn't stand it any longer and asked her, "Are you my mommy?" No one had thought to tell Carol that her mother only spoke Chinese, but the communication came through. They cried in each other's arms. Her sobbing mother apologized for never visiting her at Ming Quong. She had remarried, however, and her husband insisted she relinquish her past life and never see her child. Nevertheless, they visited secretly and became very close. As Carol said, "She loved me, and I loved her." Still, whenever they met in public, Carol's mother pretended not to know her, in submission to her husband's wishes. Carol's children, who at first delighted in finding out they had a grandma, were never acknowledged in public.

Years later, when Carol came home from work one day, a young man was waiting for her with a bouquet of fresh flowers. It was the son she had given up for adoption! That was one of the most joyous moments of her life. To this day, Carol's newfound son and his wife and grandchildren are all close, but she never again saw the daughter she had given up.

Carol is extremely proud of all her children, and it is a joy for me to see that my first playmate has weathered her storms.

6

TWO WITNESSES

early morning
suddenly shots rang out
sisters weeping

Horrifying headlines during the early Depression years bought Haley (name changed) and her younger sister, two terrified girls aged seven and eight, to the Ming Quong Home adjacent to Mills College. The event was tragic, violent, vicious, and unprecedented. It caused such a sensational stir in the Bay Area that through the years the sisters tried to put it behind them and never talked about it. Eight members of their immediate family (including a favorite uncle) and a ranch hand were murdered by a deranged individual—all in one morning. Only by the grace of God did the perpetrator miss the sisters. Years ago, Emily, an MQ girl, gave me the newspaper to read about the killings. According to the article, the two sisters saved themselves by hiding under the bed.

I met Haley, the older sister, when I was in my teens. She was a serious, kind, hard-working, conscientious individual, who later became head nurse at a Bay Area hospital. Though I did not know her sister growing up, I met her at a reunion at the Mills Ming Quong Home. Haley eventually told me their story, with the following request: "Please don't identify my sister and me with the incident I've described."

It wasn't easy for Haley and her sister when they came to the Home. They spoke a different village dialect from others. Teachers did not seem compassionate or understanding and did not show love or affection, so the sisters were not drawn to them. The only teacher Haley liked and respected was Mrs. Chan—Chun See Nye—who led Haley to the Lord. Haley once wrote me in a letter, "We've been blessed by the Lord overwhelmingly since—and we know he has work for us to do which he will reveal to us as He sees fit at the right time." She ended the letter, "God bless!"

Haley was in her mid-80s when she passed away. I have respected her wishes to keep her anonymous in this book. In her lifetime, her very presence commanded respect. She was a stern-looking matron, and in all the years I knew her, a smile never crossed her face. One could ask, however, what did this woman have to smile about?

Haley was like a member of my extended Mock family. She and my sister had both, at different times, worked for the same Palo Alto couple as a live-in helper. Each wore a uniform and ate alone in the kitchen at meal times, responding when a hand bell at the couple's dining table summoned them. I felt this was demeaning. But this was the way life was, said Haley's boss, and the sooner the girls realized their station in life, the better off they would be. They had a "live-in education," and I would say they passed!

I had a similar experience while I was a teenager living and working in Palo Alto for about two years. My employer, Mrs. Willis (name changed), whom I liked, suddenly presented me with a uniform. I objected to wearing it, but she smiled and good-naturedly cajoled me by asking, "Isn't it a cute dress?" She prodded me to wear it for a special dinner party, and I reluctantly gave in to make her happy. I felt my employer was nicer than Haley's, since I didn't have to wear the uniform every day, and I ate dinner with the family, which included a daughter in elementary school.

Years later, however, I realized that Haley's bosses

did have a "heart." When Haley and my sister moved on in the world, the couple kept in touch and became an important factor in the girls' lives. For example, my sister held her beautiful wedding in their well-manicured garden! As for me, when I went back to visit my "family," I could sense I was not welcome: I had been a mere servant!

Later in life, my sister honored Haley by making her godmother to her son. With her horrific childhood experiences, her less-than-happy existence at the Home, and her subservient house job, she became the epitome of what the "bamboo women" represent—strength and flexibility..

My sister opposed the publishing of my first book, *Chopstick Childhood,* because of the stigma attached to orphans by society, and she expressed her feelings vehemently at a Mock family picnic. To my amazement, Haley, who thought highly of the book, came to my defense. She encouraged me along the way, and I felt blessed. I had always found it hard to relate to Haley's serious, no-nonsense demeanor, but her support made me feel validated. We became true friends. We corresponded by mail, and she even braved the long drive from the South Bay to Walnut Creek to visit me at my store. She attended all the Ming Quong reunions when I was on the organizing committee, and her younger sister joined us once. I appreciated her kind, warm presence. Soft smiles lit up her stern face. At the very last reunion she attended, her happy comment was, "This was the best reunion."

After all the years, she felt the camaraderie!

7

THE CATHOLIC JOKER

outspoken child
challenging religious ways
upsetting household

What's a Protestant? What's a Catholic? Who knows if these questions would ever have arisen at the Ming Quong Home while I was growing up there if thirteen-year-old Loretta Choy (Schauer) had not come to stay. After all, the Presbyterian Board of Missions operated the Home. All we girls knew about sectarian religion was that on Sundays we attended the Presbyterian Church. We were just regular "church-goers."

But along came Loretta, and things changed. This friendly, outgoing gal with "street smarts" educated us. We soon found out that she was not like us—she was a Catholic. She informed us we were known as "Protestants," which was news to me. Loretta was truly different, not only because of her religion, but because she told so many funny stories and jokes. Always upbeat and smiling, she was a refreshing newcomer. All of us girls liked her, but the teachers did not! She had a fiery spirit and was outspoken. Neither the teachers nor the Head of the Home intimidated her. She stood up for her rights. For example, as a Catholic, Loretta did not eat meat on Fridays. (I remember wondering what kind of a church didn't let her eat meat!) Loretta's younger sister, Lynette (see next chapter), had already been at the Home but was too young to know about the Catholic ways before Loretta arrived. After Loretta came, Lynette, too, stopped eating meat on Fridays.

Loretta was like a bolt of lightning, striking with such force that before we knew it, she was there and gone in just one short year. But in those 365 days with Loretta, we learned a lot.

She once taught me a beautiful Catholic song about Mary, Jesus's mother. This intrigued me, as our church rarely spoke of Jesus's mother, and there were certainly no songs about her. I hummed this soothing melody constantly:

Mary, help us we pray
Keep our lives free from sin

Help us when we go astray
Keep our hearts pure within ...

The chorus softly repeated, with some of the same words blended harmoniously in a meditative way. That song eased my pain about my mother's abandoning me. Loretta's arrival into my life with her music was a godsend.

Although Loretta had many jokes, I remember only one, which she told a group of us MQ girls as we trudged home from school on an unusually hot day: "A young woman was dying on the sidewalk," she began. "A Father walked by and bent down to assist her. The grateful woman cried out, 'Father, help me, for I have sinned.' The Father asked her, 'What have you done?' The dying woman mumbled, 'I'm a pro—...,' and her voice faded. The Father said, 'I can't hear you; can you speak louder?' Gasping for breath, the woman spoke again, "Father, forgive me for I have sinned. I am a prostitute!' 'Oh,' the Father sighed with relief, 'I thought you were going to say you were a Protestant!'"

Loretta laughed uproariously after telling the joke, but I didn't get it. Even after she tried to explain, I didn't see the humor. It was just too "worldly" for our sheltered upbringing at the Home. On the other hand, knowledge of these "worldly" things had been a part of Loretta's background. For me, however, this joke was an introduction to the foreign words "prostitute," "Protestant," "Catholic," and even "Father" in that context.

I wondered whether the teachers knew about this joke. We ate our early Sunday meals separately from them. On the Sunday after Loretta told the joke, we heard a burst of laughter coming from the teachers' dining area. The uproar surprised us. What were they talking about? Had they gotten wind of the joke? And did they understand it and think it was funny?

In reality, that joke was somewhat representative of what Loretta had witnessed in her life before coming to us. As Loretta explained, her mother was a Chinese opera singer. Exuding glamour, her mom became quite famous in the United States and in Cuba, where there was a sizeable Chinese community that supported Chinese opera. She was a very attractive woman with a full mouth, large, sultry, dreamy eyes, and a very generous figure. She was also gutsy, an American-born woman who not only mastered Chinese opera, but became a star.

Unfortunately, Loretta's mother was not the "mothering type." She would have children and leave them where she had them. Perhaps circumstances forced these decisions on her, but Loretta never knew the reasons behind her mother's actions.

Loretta met her younger sister, Lynette, for the first time at around ten or eleven years old. Loretta lived with their maternal grandmother in San Francisco. Lynette, who was at MQ, went for a brief visit to the grandmother, and met Loretta there. The sisters did not see one another again until their mother decided to gather all her children together and make a home for them with her second husband, a musician and father of Loretta's half-brother. So Lynette left MQ at age eight. Loretta's full brother, who was living at the Chung Mei Home, also moved in. Loretta moved from her grandmother's, and her half-brother came from his (paternal) grandmother's. They all joined together to start life with their mother. It lasted one whole year.

During that year, Loretta's mom performed her gigs and made her recordings. Then suddenly she said she had to leave for New York. She sent the boys to Chung Mei and hired Darlene, a live-in white woman with a two-year-old child, to look after Lynette and Loretta.

Darlene, it turned out, was the mistress of Bock Hing's bodyguard, Bucky Wong. Bock Hing was a notorious racketeer and owner of 1940s San Francisco gambling houses. Bucky was married, and when Darlene wasn't seeing him, she started hooking—in Loretta's house! Before long, Loretta began taking care of everyone: Darlene, Darlene's two-year-old, Lynette, and herself. She had no way to reach her mother in New York to tell her of the sorry state of affairs at home. There seemed to be no alternative. She weighed the possibility of going back to her grandmother's, but that seemed out of the question. Loretta's uncle, his wife, and two new babies now lived in the grandmother's one-bedroom Chinatown apartment.

Staying with Darlene under the existing circumstances was not an option, either. Loretta took Lynette by the hand, walked her over to Cameron House, knocked on the door, and said to the first person she saw, "We need to be taken care of." She was thirteen years old, and that was how she landed at MQ.

She didn't last long at Ming Quong, however. After a year, Miss Musgrave, the last Head of the Ninth Street Home, decided that as practicing Catholics, Loretta and Lynette were too disruptive for the Presbyterian home. She sent them off to the Catholic Stanford Home in Sacramento, where Loretta stayed until graduating from high school. Due to her young age, Lynette did not fit in at Sacramento and was eventually placed in a foster home.

Loretta's mother died at the age of fifty-two. As Loretta said, "She never had a home to call her own; her relationships with men were destructive; and, in the end, she did not get the respect from her children that she wanted most of all. Despondent in the last year of her life, she suffered from sleeplessness. She got hooked on sleeping pills and accidentally overdosed on them."

In 1999, Loretta phoned me to say she couldn't attend a Ming Quong reunion I was helping to organize. I was disappointed but told her my plans to have a nickname game and asked if she remembered any of the girls' nicknames. She did, indeed! Harlan, Loretta's former roommate, whose own nickname was "Heartless," had named Loretta "Pie-Face!" "But why?" I asked. Before she could answer, I realized why—Loretta did have a round, rather flat face. Leave it to Harlan to have noticed.

Loretta reminded me of another contribution by Harlan—Mrs. Lee's nickname, "Cherry-Nose," for her small, red nose. I then mentioned the astounding fact that Mrs. Lee would be one hundred years old in January 2000. Quick-witted as ever, Loretta came back with, "Only the good die young!"

"Oh, Loretta," I laughed. "You are so bad. No wonder you were kicked out of the Home!"

Today, Loretta and her husband, Dick Schauer, a retired California Court of Appeals judge, have two homes, and they travel extensively. I don't mean a once-a-year vacation: In one year they visited at least five countries! No other MQ gal has been such a daring globetrotter. Once Loretta rode a camel edging down a steep slope. She made it, but one misstep would have been the end of her and the camel! Loretta's correspondence from Hawaii featured an impressive letterhead from the Kona Kua U'a Hotel, a vacation resort condo she once owned on the Big Island. In one of her first letters to me, she jokingly wrote, "You can see my husband is a kept man!"

In the fall of 2006, Loretta and Dick surprised me by showing up at my store and taking me and my son, Jim, out for Chinese food. They are the most generous couple. After every Ming Quong reunion, they have treated a gang of us to dinner.

Loretta and Dick had a son, a mortgage broker, who, sadly, died. They also have two beautiful daughters, both of whom are in the medical profession. One is a medical doctor with her own practice. She is the type of doctor everyone wishes for, as she truly cares about her patients. Before she entered private practice, she worked at a hospital where her father was once rushed to the emergency room. Because she already knew the intricacies of his case, she was able to save his life. When I heard this story, I turned to haiku to convey my feelings about the dynamics of the scenario:

in love and faith
our child became
a woman of hope

Their other daughter is a dentist married to a leading orthodontist. This son-in-law has a rock group in which all the musicians are dentists. It's called "OPEN WIDE." Dick said, "He makes more money than the whole family combined, but he enjoys his music more!"

When Dick goes fishing, he catches twenty or more tuna at a time. There's no way he could cart all that tuna home for Loretta to cook. So what does he do with his catch? He trades it at the fishery for canned tuna, and the cannery slaps on a special label— "Albacore, caught by rod and reel by Dick Schauer. "Because I love tuna, they sent me a case. Delicious!

Today Loretta feels lucky in her life. She said all of us bear scars from the past, and while it took her a long time to heal from her childhood, her scars are barely visible these days. I would say her guardian angel has always been with her, and her friends have been the fortunate recipients!

So now, Loretta and I are opening a sandwich shop in Pismo Beach, a great little beach town. I know we'll do so well in that quaint resort area that we'll have to recruit former MQ girls who want to join in the fun to run the place.

We're so excited.We booked OPEN WIDE to play at our grand opening!

Is this all a joke?

Ask Loretta! (But remember, she's the "joker"!)

LITTLE FON YUN

do I look like her
blonde, blue eyes and all—or
do I look like them?

According to Lynette Choy (Gin), who is Loretta's younger sister, I reprimanded her on her first day at the Ming Quong Home! We older girls were in the playroom waiting for the dining room to open. Lynette and other little girls ran around playing, screaming, and making lots of noise. I yelled, *"Mo cho . . . Lynette, Nay tim!"* (Translation: Be quiet . . . Lynette, you, too!")

Lynette remembers these words as the first ever spoken to her in Chinese. Oddly, she understood, probably just by getting the context. She was very scared. This was the first time anyone had ever yelled at her! From then on, she tried to "be good and quiet" around all the girls who had been at Ming Quong longer.

I didn't realize until she told me when we were adults that I had been Lynette's first unforgettable Chinese teacher! I'm amazed that back then I spoke Chinese well enough and with such force that Lynette obeyed! To this day, any undue noise annoys me, and Lynette relating this incident confirms that this is simply a part of my makeup! In addition, with thirty-five girls at MQ, everyone learned pretty quickly to speak up when something annoyed her. That's how we survived!

Lynette's mother had three children by age nineteen, all by the same father. At the time of Lynette's birth, her older sister, Loretta, lived with their grandmother in San Francisco Chinatown. A Chinese woman in Stockton cared for her brother, Orin. When Lynette was born in Sacramento, her father was in prison for reasons she never knew. Her mother gave birth to her at home alone on December 24, 1937. Imagine an immature nineteen-year-old feeling helpless and incapable of caring for two children, aged three and two. Then it's Christmas Eve, and here comes a newborn baby.

Lynette was two weeks old when her mother left her in the care of Mr. and Mrs. Cole, a white couple in Ventura, California. She never knew why her mom chose this specific couple to care for her as an infant, but her life with "Mama and Papa" was safe and secure.

She spent her infant and toddler years as an "only child," much loved and most likely very spoiled. She has childhood photos in which she is always clean and impeccably dressed—with tons of dolls. She has vague memories of her life as a one-year-old and remembers being happy and content.

While with the Coles in a white neighborhood, Lynette was never aware of being Chinese. She assumed she was a *fon yun* with blond hair and blue eyes like her playmates! It never occurred to her that she looked different.

Often at bedtime, Mrs. Cole showed her a photo of a woman holding her and said, "That's your mother." Lynette doesn't remember having any reaction; feelings toward her "real" mom were indifferent at the time.

Her first conscious memory of her real mother was when her mom and Tim Dong (her mother's second husband) came to Ventura to take her away from Mama Cole. Only five years old, Lynette kicked and screamed for her "Mama" as they put her into a car. After a long ride, they arrived at Ming Quong, Los Gatos, where her mother left her. Did she hold her or say good-bye? If she did, Lynette doesn't remember.

After being brought up as an "only child," Lynette was suddenly surrounded at MQ by little girls who were her round-the-clock playmates. She noticed that all the little girls had dark hair and dark eyes. They all looked just like her—and she like them! Yet she still didn't know that the way they looked had a name: "Chinese." Her first awareness of being Chinese was when Mrs. Lee (as she was known then) taught Chinese language at MQ. She taught them to count to ten and to sing "Jesus Loves Me" in Chinese. She inspired them to be proud to be Chinese.

Lynette wasn't aware she had an older sister (Loretta) or older brother (Orin). Loretta still lived with their grandmother on Commercial Street in San Francisco Chinatown. Lynette visited there when she was five or six years old and met her sister for the first time.

Lynette stayed at Ming Quong until she was eight or nine. At that point, her mother decided to gather up her children to "live as a family under one roof" at Ross Alley in San Francisco. Living together as a family was a "first ever" for all of them and quite a novel experience. The family at Ross Alley consisted of their mother and step-father, Tim Dong; their half-brother, Ronald Dong; Loretta; Orin; and Lynette. Their biological father was long gone. Lynette believes he was serving in the U.S. Army in the Panama Canal. Life at Ross Alley as a family unit was short-lived. It lasted about a year.

Unlike many of the MQ girls and Chung Mei boys who were orphaned or half-orphaned, Lynette and her siblings had two living, breathing parents. However, she doesn't remember them ever visiting, taking them on "outings," or communicating with them in any way while they were in the Homes.

Lynette believes her parents were the ultimate losers. When she and her siblings became mature adults, they began to understand their parents' irresponsible natures, weaknesses, and frailties. Their mother and father never gained the love or respect from the children they created together. Lynette believes they were painfully aware of this fact and that it haunted them to their dying days. For her parents, that is the saddest point of all.

Lynette married and was fortunate enough not to work outside the home while raising four sons. When divorce forced her to find employment in order to survive, her youngest was almost twelve years old. Her high-school typing skills kicked in at first. She believes that living in group homes made her an independent thinker, as evidenced by the significant positions she went on to hold:

- Producer and writer for a locally produced TV program in Los Angeles;
- Director of Communications for an advertising and PR firm in Los Angeles;

- Small Business Development Specialist, assisting minority and woman-owned businesses;
- Business development positions for an electronics firm and an architect / engineering firm;
- Legislative Deputy to (former) Speaker of the California Assembly and later to Lieutenant Governor Leo McCarthy, under Governor George Deukmejian;
- Founder of Lynne Choy Uyeda & Associates in 1984, a PR and marketing communications firm that developed and implemented campaigns for major corporations and government agencies to reach Asian-speaking consumer groups in the U.S.;
- Media Specialist for the California and Hawaii regions for the U.S. Census Bureau's "CENSUS 2000" campaign. This was Lynette's last assignment before retirement.

Flash forward fifty years or so to an MQ reunion at Mills College. Lynette was the bubbliest, most outgoing woman there. Definitely the most outrageously dressed in shocking pink—complete with a mini-skirt—she was a fashion statement of youth and vitality! She is still vibrant today. With her public relations background, she organized the largest Ming Quong/Chung Mei reunion in 2003, with over 250 alums attending.

And, there's more! She is now related to me, as she married my cousin, Henry Gin (a former Chung Mei boy)! How about that? Henry had read my first book, in which Lynette's sister, Loretta, was pictured. As we were reminiscing, he found out that Lynette was a single woman. He asked me if he should call her, and after much persuasion on my part (as he was supposedly shy), he did. And before I knew it, they were married!

THE PHOENIX

the rising phoenix
holding up the sky
with her achievements

The life of Bernice Bing, the artist nicknamed "Bingo," could be called a "rags to riches" tale, except that she ultimately didn't see a happy ending.

I first knew Bingo at the Los Gatos Home. She was about three years younger than me. She was the opposite of her younger, fair-skinned sister, Lolita, who, like a swan, was quiet and demure. These sisters, so different in appearance and personalities, were stunning women.

In 1961, my husband, Joe, and I attended Bingo's gala reception at the Batman Gallery in San Francisco. Her large abstract paintings were bold and masterful. While Joe took in her canvases, I was drawn to her spectacular centerpiece. It was a "horn of plenty" overflowing with an array of colorful autumn vegetables, which included, of all things, those dark-purple eggplants we had detested at the Home! I was mesmerized by the opulence of Bingo's work and in awe of her ingenuity. This was art on a grand scale with a glorious bohemian flair.

That day, Bingo glowed. She was in her element, and her black beret was perfect. She had won the respect of her contemporaries and was on her way to fame in the avant-garde art world.

At age twelve, Bingo had been off-beat and rebellious. An instigator, she possessed an air of defiance I'd never seen before. Like most MQ girls, she always spoke the truth no matter how it came across, but she was exceptionally outspoken. Once, when she was very angry with the Head of the Home, Miss Hayes, I heard her threaten to run away. That astounded me, as it had never occurred to anyone to do such a thing. Bingo not only thought about it, but she actually did it—and she took some other girls with her. They stayed overnight in a neighboring orchard, and when they were hungry, they simply plucked ripe fruit off the trees like Adam and Eve.

Later, Lynette, one of the runaways, told me, "The teachers did not seem overly concerned about our disappearance." To the contrary, I'm sure the teachers were overwrought, but Miss Hayes had to utilize the old Chinese characteristic of "saving face" and not letting the girls "win."

This incident happened after I had moved from Los Gatos to the Oakland Home, and I learned of it only years later. Bingo's defiance of the powers that be presaged her later role as a powerful leader and trailblazer for the arts in San Francisco. She received scholarships, honors, and awards and studied and mingled with all the great thinkers and artists of her time. Later she became director of SomArts, the South of Market arts and culture center in San Francisco.

Bingo hated the Home and for some reason felt it was to blame for the cancer death at a very young age of her sister, Lolita. Bingo shared this startling fact with me at the art show in the Batman Gallery. I was upstairs in Bingo's bedroom above the gallery, where I noticed an exquisite black-and-white painting leaning against the wall on the hardwood floor. It was a portrait of a Chinese girl, so different from the abstract works exhibited downstairs. I loved it immediately and wanted to buy it, but it was not for sale.

"Why not?" I exclaimed.

"I painted it from a book of photographs because it reminded me of Lolita," Bingo replied. She explained why she thought the Home had caused Lolita's early death. She felt that the structure at the Home was excessively rigid, and that the introverted Lolita had found it so stressful that she became ill.

I now have a copy of this very same painting hanging at home alongside my favorite black-and-white photograph of Bingo. Under each picture is a haiku I composed for her and Lolita.

Bingo and Lolita's father had a dark complexion and was very handsome. He resembled Rudolph Valentino and worked as the manager of the National Dollar Store in San Francisco. Unfortunately, he was also addicted to opium, and eventually he just disappeared.

Lolita was the image of her mother, Evalyn, a beautiful woman with a fair complexion who worked as a hat girl at the famous Forbidden City nightclub in San Francisco. At an early age, Evalyn was diagnosed with heart disease and given three months to live. She died before she was twenty-four. (Today, a fancy headdress from the famous club is on permanent display at the Ming Quong history wall in Los Gatos, courtesy of Lolita.)

One day Bingo, aged five, and Lolita, aged four, were with their mother in Oakland's Chinatown. They stopped at a corner, where their mother said to wait until she came back for them. They obeyed, and the minutes went by, then the hours went by, and their mother never returned. Finally a police officer stopped and asked why they were standing there. That's how the two heart-broken sisters became wards of the court. Bingo was subsequently placed in seventeen Caucasian foster homes before coming to Ming Quong, and occasionally she lived in San Francisco with her very traditional grandmother.

This grandmother had bound feet and was extremely cantankerous and cruel to Bingo. Alone, with no connection to either culture, and, doing poorly in a white middle-class school, Bingo withdrew into her drawings. To her surprise, her grandmother noticed and complimented her artwork. That was when Bingo realized that her art could bridge the two cultures and that she could finally communicate with others. At the age of seven, Bingo had found her life's destiny!

Lolita married at a very young age, and that status allowed her to get Bingo out of the court system and the Home. Bingo, no longer a ward, was now free to live her life!

Through the years, I occasionally read about Bingo and her artwork. Once, the San Francisco Chronicle pictured her painting on the floor of an enormous warehouse on the San Francisco waterfront. Needing more space, she became the first artist to utilize such massive quarters. Bingo dreamt large; she was limitless. A retrospective ceremony honoring her was titled, "They Hold Up Half the Sky," a take on the famous saying of Mao Zedong in China with reference to women. But I would dare to say that here in America, Bernice Bing held up the whole sky!

Bernice won the Women's Caucus for Art Lifetime Achievement Award in 1996, presented at Rutgers University by our mutual friend, Flo Oy Wong. Flo's introduction for the award spoke about Bingo's charitable work with the Wah Chings in San Francisco Chinatown. Here is Flo's speech (quoted from the Lesbian Visual Arts Magazine's 1996 article entitled, "The Tao of Bernice Bing: Her Life and Her Art"):

> During a violent phase in Chinatown when killing was rampant, Bingo established an art workshop with the Baby Wah Chings, a Chinatown gang. The program gave eleven- to thirteen-year-olds a place to channel their energies. For those efforts, Bing won recognition. In 1983, she received the Distinguished Alumni Award from the San Francisco Art Institute. In 1984, Bing was awarded the San Francisco Art Commission Award for Distinguished Work &

Achievement in Community Arts. From 1980 to 1984, she directed and established innovative programs at the South of Market Cultural Center.

In 1958, Bingo had begun studying on scholarship with Nathan Oliveira, Saburo Hasegawa, and Richard Diebenkorn at the California College of Art and Crafts in Oakland. Under Hasegawa, she changed from advertising to painting with a Zen approach, using calligraphic strokes and abstract techniques. In the crafts department, she learned the method of lost-wax casting in jewelry-making with our mutual friend, Robert Winston. In 1961 she graduated from the San Francisco Art Institute with a Master's degree in fine arts.

Bingo was a resident artist at Esalen in 1967 and was among the first to study New Age psychology and philosophy with Joseph Campbell, Alan Watts, Fritz Perls, and others. She took her artistic inspiration from varied sources, among them deKooning in art, Stein in poetry, Camus in literature, Beckett in film, and Fellini in art films.

Under Bingo's leadership, the first Asian American Festival was established in the San Francisco Civic Center. She also organized art events and programs for the city. In 1990, Bingo received the Asian Heritage Council Art Award in recognition of her talent and her efforts in support of Chinese-American cultural activities in San Francisco.

At one point after a move to Philo, near Mendocino in northern California, Bingo made an extended trip to China to renew her art and satisfy an ongoing natural longing to learn more about her ancestral roots. Ever-broadening her knowledge of art, she studied calligraphy at the Zhejiang Academy in China. She lectured Chinese students about her style of painting. To her amazement, the students easily grasped her artwork, for her bold abstracts spoke to them in terms of their own calligraphy! Bingo returned from China renewed, and she incorporated workshops with an Eastern format at her studio in peaceful Philo.

Bingo's interest in the parallel of Eastern mysticism and modern physics changed her way of painting. *The Tao of Physics*, a book by Fritjof Capra, greatly influenced her later works. She evolved from the traditional painting of only one subject, to paintings that included many different images of the same subject!

For one work, she painted forty colorful individual panels. When these separate works were merged, they formed one massive piece approximately sixteen-by-eleven feet. This was one of two parts of what she called the "quantum series." The other part of the series had ninety-nine black-and-white panels arranged in a similar manner. She used abstracts and calligraphic strokes with spontaneous images. She kept the whole picture in mind, yet she was never sure of how the finished work would look. Hanging all the paintings and seeing it all come together was an exhilarating moment. With the museum's quality lighting projected perfectly on her masterpieces, the results were spectacular. The concept was brilliant! She sold individual panels and then rearranged the remaining ones into a new picture on the wall.

Following the teachings of the Tao Te Ching, Bingo was indeed "the light in the dark." She was also one of the "radiant lights" of Ming Quong despite her dislike of the Home.

When I published *Chopstick Childhood,* Bingo drove the considerable distance from her home in Philo to attend a book reading I gave in Berkeley at the well-known East Wind Book Store. There were seven former Ming Quong residents in the audience, and we had an impromptu reunion. When Bingo waltzed in, we all yelled her name in surprise. It was the first time Bingo had seen so many Ming Quong girls since leaving the Home. She looked harried and very tired, but a bright smile lit up her entire face. She presented me with sweet-smelling narcissus from her garden, wrapped in Chinese red and yellow "cut-out" paper she had hand-cut herself.

After my reading, in which I praised my upbringing at the Ming Quong Home, Bingo said loud and clear for all to hear, "OK, Nona, now tell it like it really was!"

A second of strained silence filled the room.

When I said, "Oh, Bingo, if you had written the book, I know it would have been different," there was laughter from all of us MQ gals! It gave me a good feeling that Bingo had come, because even though she felt her experiences at the Home were negative, she at least now knew for certain that we loved her.

One of Bingo's very last exhibits was a travelling show that went across the country and eventually to China! But first it came to Walnut Creek, where I live and have my store. I attended the show on Sunday, thinking Bingo would be there. I was warmly greeted by the curator, who asked me, "Are you Bernice Bing?"

Flattered, I laughed, "Who, me?" I wrote Bingo about this mistaken identity and ended the letter by saying, "I would be proud to be you!"

The above makes Bingo sound like a Wonder Woman with unlimited endurance. That is not completely true. Many of her contemporaries did not know that Bingo had a life-threatening health problem. She was in need of a liver transplant. Although she did not have the funds, her name was placed on the waiting list at Stanford Hospital in Palo Alto, CA. A good friend who had once waited tables with her at the Old Spaghetti Factory in San Francisco saved his money for her operation. But it was too late. In 1998, Bingo passed away, just two weeks after my reading. I felt so sad that Bingo had gone through this experience by herself, with no help from me or any of the other Ming Quong girls.

I spoke at a memorial for Bingo at her beautiful new hilltop home in Philo. Even though Bingo disliked Ming Quong, her house shared much with the Home. Like an Eichler-style house, hers featured natural wood, beam ceilings, and expansive windows to drink in the view of the surrounding trees and mountains, all reminiscent of the Home. In the back yard was a new wooden deck surrounding a giant oak tree, just like one at the Ming Quong. The floral display featured amaryllis belladonnas, a favorite at the Home. To top it off, Bingo's wonderful cat roamed around freely nuzzling the guests, just like the resident cat at Ming Quong.

The deYoung Museum in San Francisco purchased Bingo's painting, "Mayacamas #6." It hangs on the main floor in one of the contemporary galleries between two canvases by Richard Diebenkorn, her former instructor. The museum store sells note cards and postcards of the work. Bingo's art continues to enlighten and inspire. She was featured in a 2008 deYoung exhibit titled "Shifting Currents," featuring Asian-American artists, and in the Stanford University Press book published in conjunction with this event. In her lifetime, Bingo didn't have the funds for her transplant at Stanford Hospital, yet since her death in 1998, her paintings sell for $30,000 at galleries and auctions worldwide.

This is ironic, sad, and poignant. Bernice Bing lives on in her legacy, rising like the phoenix.

10

THE CHOSEN PRINCESS

devastated
parents gone—what lay ahead?
a place of honor!

What would our lives have been like if we had been adopted from the Ming Quong Home to live with a loving mother and father? In my age group, which consisted primarily of "long-term" girls, we were worried and even scared by the thought of adoption. It meant we would have to leave all our childhood friends, perhaps never to see them again. Because of our common needs, our bonds were strong. In some ways, they were even stronger than those of sisters from a "regular" family. Nevertheless, we wondered what adoption would be like.

I never knew anyone who had been adopted from Ming Quong until a luncheon in the spring of 2007, where I meet Dale Andrea Wong (Lee), a tall, imposing woman who had lived at the Home more than a decade after me. The lunch featured a panel of grown-up Ming Quong girls and Chung Mei boys talking about our experiences at the Homes. Dale said, "I was one of the fortunate ones. I was adopted by foster parents who became my mom and dad, then grandma and grandpa to my children."

As fortunate as I've always felt that the Home was there for me, I was excited to hear, over seventy years later, what it felt like to have a mother and father and to feel their love! The whole story Dale told me later was a little more complicated than I anticipated:

Like many Chinese families, Dale's birth parents had owned a grocery store, which made it possible for them to live comfortably on Vallejo Street near San Francisco's Chinatown. Life was sweet, briefly. And then tragedy struck.

While driving the family car one day, Dale's father suffered a major heart attack and hit another car. He died, and Dale's mother—whose first husband had also died—lost the grocery store paying damages for the accident. "Mom slowly sank into a state of depression," Dale said, "a condition for which, at the time, little or no medical help was available. Even if it had been, a woman who spoke no English and had no financial support would not have received it."

Facing destitution, Dale's mother felt inadequate to care for both Dale and an older daughter by her first husband. Through friends, she learned about Ming Quong. "She struggled to do the best she could to care for me," Dale said. "Mom finally agreed that Ming Quong was perhaps the answer, not only for herself but mainly for me. In spite of her depression, Mom had the clarity of mind to know that it was difficult enough to meet her own needs, let alone to provide for a five-year-old daughter."

And so, one bright and sunny day in 1951, Dale found herself at Ming Quong. By day's end, she realized she was staying behind when her mother left. "With the innocence of a child, I clung to my mom, pleading with her through tears not to leave me," Dale said. "What had I done to make her abandon me? All I wanted was to be with her. Who was going to take care of me now that both Dad and Mom had left me? This was the first of many nights that I cried myself to sleep. I always hoped that I was having a very bad nightmare and that when I awoke in the morning, Mom would take me home and tell me she had made a terrible mistake."

Hearing about Dale's abandonment brought back my own memories of fears and anguish. In fact, I believe such shared experience amplifies the strength of orphanage bonding. Fortunately, kids are resilient. With the passage of each day when her mother failed to show up, Dale became reconciled to her new home and adjusted to Ming Quong.

Dale remembers fun times with her new "sisters" playing kick-the-can, exploring the Home's grounds, and finding places to hide. As she said, "I could let my imagination fly beyond the boundaries of gravity to a place where people loved me and held me when I was hurt, sick, or feeling lonely. I was too young to realize anything was amiss with my situation. My mother and older sister visited about once a year to check on my status. As I grew older, the good-byes were no longer tearful or heartbreaking. In fact, they seemed natural."

Most Ming Quong girls had a favorite teacher. Dale's was the Burmese house mother, Adelaide Martin, who remained her lifelong friend. Miss Martin had overcome extreme adversity in her life. She walked with a limp, the result of early hardship suffered when she and many other Burmese fled on foot over the mountains to avoid being captured by the invading Japanese. Dale regularly visited her in Napa until she died in 1985.

Dale's childhood took another sharp turn in the mid-fifties when a couple, John and Fern Schmidt, came to Ming Quong. Concerned for the welfare of Chinese girls, the Schmidts invited some girls to visit them on weekends in San Francisco. Eventually, they chose Dale as their foster daughter, although her birth mother refused to let her be formally adopted. "I became their 'princess' for a while because they had no other children. I received many hugs and displays of love from my foster parents." During the next few years, five more children were added to the family: one Samoan, three Koreans, and Faye, another Chinese girl from the Los Gatos Ming Quong Home. Like Dale, Faye was not formally adopted, but the Schmidts always treated them as their own daughters, as integral parts of the family. The Schmidt relationship continued throughout the years. Dale got together with them on holidays at their home until the death of "Mom" in 1990 and "Dad" in 2002.

Dale married in 1967 and had four children and four grandchildren. When her oldest grandchild, Samantha, was six years old, Dale recalled that she had been about that age when her mother left her at Ming Quong. "It's hard to imagine leaving my granddaughter in a strange environment to be brought up by strangers," she reflected.

Once again, I felt a bond with Dale. While writing, I always noticed mothers with a little daughter of two or three years old, the age at which I entered Ming Quong. I knew what it would be like for this toddler to be separated from her mother, her best friend. I wondered how my mother could bear to leave me at the orphanage.

What heartbreaking sadness we all knew—our mothers included. Yet time did heal us. As Dale said, "It's taken over sixty years for me to fully appreciate the impact of Ming Quong on my life. We had lessons to learn from living at MQ with each other. We each chose how we responded to this experience, as we do to every experience in life. We can let it affect our lives—either positively or negatively." For a long while, Dale felt like a victim: "I've had a difficult time finding myself—not only in regards to my self-esteem, but also in learning how to relate to others without being a 'victim.' But that is in the past, and I am not a victim anymore." Now Dale's positive words are, "We are Ming Quong girls, and we are wonderful." And I agree!

Dale was with the South San Francisco Unified School District for twenty-six years and retired in 2011. She has served as a part-time classroom aide, a high-school registrar, and an executive assistant to one of the district superintendents. In retirement, she is babysitting her one-year-old grandson twice a week.

Although Dale was never legally adopted, she felt wholly accepted into the hearts of her foster parents. Thus, my "what if" question was answered:

When the feeling of love is truly felt
The heart will respond
And when the heart speaks
The truth is revealed

Yes, Dale was fortunate, for she was, indeed, "The Chosen Princess."

11

ONE PRETTY FLOWER

Qui Mei
the gift of a Chinese name
fulfils destiny

A natural beauty, Edna Lee (Christman) was athletic and daring and possessed an adventuresome spirit. She was well-liked by all. We called her a "tomboy." Always the first to try something new, she once jumped up on the middle of our giant teeter-totter and challenged everyone to climb aboard while she balanced herself. Laughing, we clamored aboard. Suddenly the heavy board creaked and split. She jumped clear, as the rest of us tumbled off, laughing. We were in trouble. Our punishment: the teeter-totter was never repaired.

Edna had the one and only bicycle at the Home, a gift from her mother. Generous with this coveted, blue-and-white treasure, Edna let everyone ride it, which resulted in multiple bang-ups and plenty of flat tires. Because she owned the bike, it was her responsibility to walk it down to the gas stationto pump air into the tires, even on sweltering summer days. Poor Edna dripped with perspiration, but she never complained. From our vantage point on the hillside, we would see the lone figure trudging up the hill with her bike and let out loud cheers, "Yea, Edna's back!"

Edna's life before Ming Quong was marked by her father's physical abuse of her mother. As Edna stated, "My father was a gambler who did menial jobs. Mother worked in the sweatshops and often had to bring home work she could not finish. Before I could walk, she often took me to work with her and placed me in a box of excelsior near the motor of her sewing machine to keep me warm while she sewed her allotment of clothing. My father was a very jealous man, and when my mother had to work late to finish her quota of garments, he physically abused her and accused her of 'messing around.' On one occasion, we six children were all standing in the doorway of the one-bedroom apartment. As mother came up the steep stairs, my father struck her several times with a rolling pin, causing her to tumble all the way down the stairs. I do not remember which hurt her more, the fall or the rolling pin. All I remember was fear."

After numerous beatings, Edna's mother found the strength to leave her abusive life. Edna continued: "I do not know how many times these beatings occurred, but I think after the rolling pin incident my mother decided to take us kids and leave my father. Fortunately, she knew about Donaldina Cameron's mission of rescuing children in need. She left the six of us standing in front of Cameron House on Sacramento Street in San Francisco. She knew we would be taken in and placed in appropriate homes. My mother then went into hiding, fearing for her life. My father, who belonged to a tong, sent word out to find and kill her for causing him embarrassment and loss of face in the eyes of his tong association. With my mother in hiding, her friends managed to find a husband for her. He would provide her protection from my father's tong" (a "tong" is a male-dominated association of men with the same surname, like Lee or Sing. Back in the 1800s, tong wars were common, as the tongs fought over Chinatown's lucrative gambling and female-trafficking businesses. Now there are only five tongs left on the West Coast and two on the East Coast, all legitimate business associations).

Edna entered the Home in 1939 with her younger sister, Nora. Their older sister, Pansy, preceded them by a few months. Edna has vivid memories of the long pathway leading up to the main building at her new home at Ming Quong. As she recalls, "We were to walk that very same path many, many times. Little did we know that this would be our home for many years to come. I personally feel that this was the happiest and most care-free time of my life. We were taught to obey the teachers, to be neat and clean in our person, and to help with the many chores that such a large household required."

At Edna's new home, she had trees to climb and acres to explore in fresh air and healthy sunshine. There were no more crowded streets teeming with harried shoppers and providing nowhere to play. Gone were the damp fog and cold weather. But probably the most luxurious benefit was sleeping in one's own bed without siblings! I understand her bliss. At one time in my teens, my cousins and I visited their father in San Francisco Chinatown. He lived in one tiny room, which he had divided by a hanging sheet into two even smaller rooms, a kitchen and a bedroom. This was my first glimpse at tenement living, and I tried to imagine an entire family, such as Edna's, crammed into such small living quarters. This visit awakened my senses to life in Chinatown.

Despite her improved environment, there were still challenges for Edna. "I vividly remember our first day at grammar school," she recalled. "Miss Reber, the cook for the Home, left my little sister and me at the front gate and told us to go on in. There we were, two scared little children, standing alone on that long stretch of walkway up to the main school building, which seemed so large. I remember a flagpole in the middle of that walkway. We were so frightened that we just held on to each other, hugging and crying at the same time. I wondered why our big sister, Pansy, did not come out to ease our fears and show us where to go. Eventually someone led us to the office, where the initial preliminaries were taken care of, and we were placed in our separate classes."

Some may wonder why Miss Reber didn't guide them in the right direction that first day, and I believe she probably felt they would be fine because "they had each other." After all, despite her busy morning schedule, she had taken the time to drive them to school before her usual, massive, grocery-shopping chores. I'm sure she was not completely aware of their anxiety. I had also been fearful my first day at kindergarten. I was by myself and scared, so Miss Reber kindly walked me in. But even with her gentle smile and coaxing, I still cried!

During World War II, we were too young to know any details of the war besides "black out" nights when all the lights had to be turned off so the enemy could not spot us from the air. But one memory was clear for Edna:

"My three brothers lived at the Chung Mei Home. My oldest brother, Howard, was drafted into the army as soon as he graduated from high school at age 18. I felt so proud when he came to see us at Ming Quong before he was shipped to Europe. He was so handsome in his army uniform. Unfortunately, I did not get to know him well. Six months later, he died in Germany. Those days are a blur to me. I only know that my brother was dead and that he was killed in action."

At the Home, our teacher, Mrs. Lee, told us that the brother of some of the girls had died in the war. We wondered who it was, as we had never known anyone who died. We prayed for the brother's family in prayer group. When we lifted our heads, we saw a crying Nora. All of us were teary-eyed.

In their teens, Edna and Nora moved to the Oakland Ming Quong on Ninth and Oak Streets. They spent a year or so there, attending Lincoln School. Eventually, the girls returned to their mother. As Edna recalled, "One day, as I walked past the administrator's office at the Home, I overheard Miss Higgins having a telephone conversation. She mentioned my mother's name and said they would send someone to her house to see whether it was appropriate for my sister and me to return to her. I don't know how I knew what I needed to do, but I immediately ran to a telephone booth near the park. I placed a precious dime in the pay phone and called my mother collect to alert her to the fact that someone was coming to check her out.

"But nothing happened. Years later, I learned from Pansy that we were not allowed to go home because my mother's second husband had the same name as a known drug user or dealer, and the home was deemed an unsuitable environment for young girls. Only after the death of mom's second husband were we allowed to live in her house in Stockton, California.

"Our return home was exciting, but full of new experiences. At Ming Quong, we were used to doing household chores, but going to a new school involved different skills. We had to learn bus schedules, remember lunch money, and purchase our own gym and school clothes. All these matters had been taken care of for us by the Ming Quong Home.

"Returning home meant an additional financial burden for my mother. With three more mouths to feed, she had to work longer hours at the laundry. I felt a huge void in my life because she was unable to spend any time with us girls. My sisters had their own circle of friends, and I felt very lonely. I was not that interested in school, and at the age of fifteen, I got married. Years later, I realized

I had married partly to take the financial burden off my mom."

It was just like Edna to put other people's welfare before her own. At the time, I heard from an older MQ girl that Miss Higgins approved of Edna's marriage at such a young age. Miss Higgins reportedly commented that, "Edna is so wild and pretty. Marriage will tame her. She will be safer married."

I remember commenting, "Humph! Miss Higgins said that?" To me, that was not parental thinking! But, of course, Edna was not the Home's responsibility anymore.

At the MQ reunions, I noticed that Edna went by the name of Qui Mei. Curious, I asked her about the name change. She only smiled with no reply. So I moved on and kidded her about the word 'Qui' which means "naughty" in Cantonese. We laughed. Sometime later, I asked Nora why Edna had changed her name. Her response, "Qui Mei was Edna's Chinese name, which according to Edna's sister-in-law, means Pretty Flower."

Edna had her first child at sixteen, and by age twenty-two, she had four children. She divorced at twenty-three and eventually married four times. She had eight grandchildren and five great grandchildren. Pretty Flower sowed her seeds and blossomed! I'm sure her huge family was full of gorgeous Qui Meis beautifying the scenery, all imbued with her energy and wonderful spirit. Now I know why Edna had not translated the meaning of her Chinese name for me: She had been too modest.

Sadly, Edna passed away in 2003, shortly after a Ming Quong and Chung Mei reunion. That was the last time I saw her, and her final request for me was to sign a few more copies of *Chopstick Childhood* for her to give away as gifts. I felt honored.

I'll always think of Edna's sentiments about the Home: "Ming Quong was the happiest and most carefree time of my life." That is the finest tribute one could bestow. She was blessed. We were blessed.

12

PRETTY JENNY LEE

best friends, ever
like sisters, yet closer
always proud "twins"

The 1993 Ming Quong Home reunion on the Mills College campus was winding down. It had been a day filled with nostalgia for many of the women, all in their 70s and 80s, who had once lived at this beautiful site. Most of them had returned for the first time, and now they were seeing their childhood home through new eyes. It still looked elegant, reminiscent of the house of an aristocrat from Old China! Missing, however, were the two powerful-looking foo dogs that had graced both sides of the Home's grand entrance.

While the MQ girls and their guests meandered around the grounds, Jenny Lee (Wong) and I were in the Home's huge dining room, laughing and chatting.

Suddenly the friendly voice of Genevieve, an older Ming Quong woman, called out, "Hello, Pretty Jenny Lee!" Jenny blushed, and I remembered that the older girls at the Los Gatos Home had called her by that name. Actually, she received that nickname from the teacher, Miss Hayes, who was the Head of the Home. Jenny was lucky, because Miss Hayes often hurt girls with her remarks. She told one older girl she wasn't pretty and would never have dates, and she unfavorably compared my flat body to that of another, curvaceous girl.

Had Genevieve not reminded me of the nickname, this chapter title would have been titled, "My Sister, My Twin." That's how close Jenny and I became. We dubbed ourselves "the twins" in our teen years and were alike in so many ways.

Jenny was the youngest of three sisters. She, Florence, and Bernice lived in West Oakland until their mother died of TB and their father placed them in the Los Gatos Home in 1938. They were well-liked and adjusted easily into orphanage living.

Jenny was five, a year older than me, and we were both in the Nursery group. Though we became good friends, one of my first memories of her was not a happy one. I was a slow eater, especially when we had mush for breakfast. One school morning, I was the last one to leave the house. As I ran down the hill, I was relieved to see Jenny and two other girls ahead of me. "Jenny," I yelled, "Wait for me." She stopped, smiled, and waited for a moment, but then all of a sudden they sprinted off. I was completely surprised by this action. In desperation I yelled more loudly. Once again they stopped, but then they ran off again. This time it was worse, for they all laughed at me! I was stunned, but I just kept running, with tears streaming down my face. Nevertheless, we became good friends afterward. Most of our life at the Home was playtime, and hurts dissipated quickly.

Every Saturday night after dinner, all the girls and teachers assembled in the living room, the most beautiful room in the house, for prayer time. We sang our favorite hymns while Miss Reber accompanied us on the piano. Whoever ran the fastest to the living room won the privilege of sitting on one of the two prized, wicker rocking chairs reserved for the Nursery girls. Jenny was one of the lucky girls who always seemed to win.

This weekly get-together was special, as all week long we were kept with only our own age groups. On Saturdays we got to be with the older girls, whom we admired. Except for those nights, the living room was reserved for visiting guests or parents. This "showroom" had a large picture window with a view of the surrounding mountains and

San Jose in the far distance. On Sunday nights, the teachers dined there by themselves without having to attend to us. They treated themselves to a deluxe salad complete with avocado. It must have been a real luxury for them.

One time, a Caucasian couple wanted to adopt Jenny, and she wanted to be adopted, but her father would not consent. In contrast, most girls never wanted to be adopted and leave their friends.

At one point Jenny's father could not afford the Home's monthly expenses for the three sisters, so they all moved back to his house in Oakland. The county paid for most of the long-term girls' room and board, and had Jenny's father known to ask the Home for help, the Presbyterian Church's National Board of Missions would have subsidized his payments. In any event, Jenny was devastated at having to move. She missed the Home so much that she begged her father to let her come back. His house rarely had food, and there was no one around all day, since her sisters went to work. A nearby restaurant owner knew about Jenny's living conditions and fed her so she would not starve. Jenny continued to beg to return to Ming Quong, and, finally, her father agreed to have her come back part-time. She joined us during fruit season when we cut apricots and prunes on various farms in the early mornings to earn our monthly allowances.

When Jenny returned, the teachers felt there was something wrong with her. They asked her whether everything was okay. If not, they said, she could continue to live there instead of going back to her father's home. However, Jenny was scared to tell them the truth about the living conditions at her father's house because she thought she would never see her sisters again.

In my early teens, I moved to the Oakland Home. Jenny was once again living at her father's house, but we attended Lincoln School and Oakland High together, and it was during this time that we became really close and began calling ourselves "twins." We once even dressed as twins in white peasant blouses, black flats, dark-green-print dirndl skirts, and a wide sash that tied in the back with a perky bow. We were happy, especially considering our limited budget. We always carefully shopped for bargains at stores like Lerner's.

That day we strolled around Oakland's Lake Merritt. Cars slowed down to look at us "twins," and people we passed seemed amused. Heads turned as we walked by. When we reached Chinatown, we saw the familiar scenes: elderly men chatting, others immersed in newspapers, and others staring off into space as they replayed old memories. When they saw us, they all stopped their routines and raised their heads in surprise. Then whistles came our way from "older" (out of high school) guys in Chinatown. We giggled and blushed, as they seemed so "worldly" and handsome to our eyes.

When Jenny and I were in the eighth grade, she occasionally brought me a prized treat from a relative's Chinatown grocery store. Although this treat only cost a penny, it was very hard to obtain, as the stores were always sold out. This coveted sweet was a huge piece of bubble gum in a bright, pink wrapper. Oh, we loved it! We chewed and snapped the gum until we felt our jaws would wear out. Laughing with glee, we blew giant bubbles that exploded messily all over our faces.

Sadly, our real-life "bubble" soon burst, and our world exploded around us. At about age sixteen, life suddenly changed. I left Ming Quong for a live-in job in Palo Alto and later shared an Oakland apartment with other MQ girls. Having been sheltered and protected most of my life, I was now on my own with the trusting nature imbued in me by the Home. Jenny left her father's home at age seventeen after a heated argument. He had regularly abused her physically, hitting her for no apparent reason. I had introduced her to Dave, a man I had once dated, and she accepted his proposal of marriage, feeling she had nowhere else to go. It was the same for me. I did have second thoughts about marrying Joe, but

I had promised another girl she could have my space in the apartment, and I could not break my promise to her. I went ahead and married.

In the beginning, both Jenny and I felt secure. We were married, the ultimate goal for a girl at that time. We had husbands to care and provide for us and to be our best friends for the rest of our lives. What could be better? The Ming Quong teachers had done their job well. Society smiled down on us! At the Home we had been taught to observe Christian ways: to be kind and fair, to keep our promises, to obey the teachers, and to respect authority. As a result, the marriage vows were sacred to us. We honored and obeyed our husbands, even though it later came to be against our better judgement most of the time.

Both of our husbands became possessively jealous and insecure. Whenever they were away from us, they imagined us flirting with other men, or worse, while we were just being ourselves, enjoying life. We came to understand that we did not have fairy-tale marriages, but in our naïveté, we thought that things would change if our husbands just loved us enough! But problems multiplied. Soon we lost friends because our husbands would not allow us to see them, and our lives sank into submissiveness. We were like "slaves" in our marriages, subject to our husbands' demands!

Dave's mother had a Chinese restaurant. Jenny, who had never cooked a day in her life, was literally thrust into the kitchen with her mother-in-law, where she quickly learned all about the restaurant business. Dave, a contractor who built many beautiful homes, was, unfortunately, an alcoholic. He lost many contracts because of it, and he became mentally cruel to Jenny.

Once Jenny ventured to say that ninety percent of the Ming Quong girls' marriages must be like ours! I felt very sad to think that could be true. I hated to think of Donaldina Cameron's work coming to that. She and the other dedicated missionaries who gave their hearts and souls for their "daughters" had fought for them to be free from enslavement of any kind. In some ways, it had been easier to address the type of enslavement that existed in the Gold Rush days. Some of the Ming Quong girls blame the teachers for not giving us better guidance in social intercourse and life skills. They should have taught us to seek men who were secure with themselves, who lived each day in positive ways. Fortunately, they *had* taught us the suppleness of "bamboo mentality." We knew how "to compromise, to yield, but to move forward unbroken," as stated by the writer, Maggie Oster. And we are very thankful for that positive trait!

Jenny and Dave had two daughters and a son. Tragically, the younger daughter died from an illness at a young age, and the son passed away in 2007 from a heart attack. I felt such sadness, but, as Jenny said, she has many wonderful memories of them.

Jenny finally divorced Dave. Still married, I asked her, "How could you be brave enough to do that?" Her reply: "I had to do it. His cruelty was unbearable. When I divorced him it was the most carefree day of my life!" Dave has since died. Jenny went on to work at an electronics company for twenty-five years. She also worked for NASA on the Apollo program and was one of ten employees who assembled the antenna for the first rocket to go to the moon. She met the astronaut, Walter Cunningham, and received a White House certificate thanking her for her participation.

I stuck with my marriage, and it eventually became a good one. Joe had a great interest in psychology and became a social worker. He felt deep concern for man's inhumanities to man. He became aware of his negative behavior and went to a psychiatrist for help. In turn, I saw a therapist, and in the end, we joined a married-couple's group. The sessions helped, and life became liveable. Joe actually felt very sad about my background as an orphan, and during our life together, he eventually imbued me with the confidence that is part of my life today. His death in 2003, after forty-nine years of marriage, was the saddest I had ever experienced. He was a troubled soul but a kind one, and I am a wiser person for having lived through life with him. Still, the loss of Joe, though profound, also freed my spirit.

Today Jenny and I agree we are content never to marry again, despite the fact that married people are healthier and live longer. I once posed the question to Jenny, "What if? Just what if you met someone; you never know …"

"Nah," we laughed, and our voices trailed off. I don't think it will happen for either of us "twins."

Jenny and I also agree that Ming Quong was one of the happiest times of our lives. So many of the MQ girls say the very same thing, which may sound surprising in view of the generally negative connotation of orphanage living. Yet, Ming Quong definitely did something right! Once again, I commend the teachers and all involved in our lives there. Jenny said, "I am grateful for the Home. You can imagine how I would have turned out otherwise. I would have been very poor with no education."

Life is a joyful experience intertwined with friends, and Jenny remains my friend and "twin" in many ways.

13

THE SONGBIRD

the girl who likes opera
refuses to sing
at Forbidden City
by jerry ball

Lonnie Lee, now in her early nineties, is well known for her beautiful singing voice. She came to the Ming Quong Home as a three-year-old. "My full name is Eva Lon Tom Lee. My father owned a cafeteria business in Los Angeles and could not care for me after my mother left us," Lonnie told me, "so I was placed in the Tooker Home," an orphanage for very young Chinese children in Oakland. The Tooker Home was a two-story Victorian house donated by a couple of dedicated sisters.

Even as a child, people constantly sought this petite singer with her soft smile and demure ways. The teachers at the Ming Quong Home recognized her talent and knew that this winsome child had the ability to share her gift with others. They prepared her for performances for guests and potential contributing visitors. As Lonnie said, "I remember being put in nooks and corners of the Ming Quong Home adjacent to Mills College to learn a song in one hour." Though under pressure, she was quick to absorb the music. I marvelled at her learning skills, and her face brightened for a split second, but then she modestly stated, "It was easy. I was just a child. I learned fast."

At one time, she and three contemporaries were chosen to pay homage to an MQ benefactor, Captain Robert Dollar of the Dollar Steamship Lines, who donated the land adjacent to Mills College.

I vividly remember seeing the picture of this historic celebration in books about Donaldina Cameron. I lingered at this photo, studying the girls' cute little faces, all smiling and happy. Then I checked out the Captain's pleasant expression. But one thing distracted me—Captain Dollar's goatee! It looked exactly like the beard of the gruff, old billy goat we read about in books at school! I had never seen a goatee like that, and I'm pretty certain the singers had not, either. Like any curious young girls, they would have wanted to ask questions about his beard, but they would have resisted. MQ girls had perfect manners. The teachers had taught them to respect their elders,and they would not have giggled or stared.

I was excited to hear more about this historical happening from an actual participant, but Lonnie would not talk about it further. Iwas puzzled by her air of indifference. Was she bored? Did my questions hit a sore spot? Or was she just tired of answering a question she'd been asked all her life? I sensed these questions conjured up negative thoughts for a child who was unable to be like her carefree MQ friends, who played outdoors while she was confined in a corner of the house doing what was expected of her—rehearsing.

Being gifted and in the limelight ran in Lonnie's family. Her older brother, Milton Tom, was the "poster boy" for the Chung Mei Home. A well-publicized photograph of young Milton and Dr. Sheperd, the Chung Mei administrator, appeared in many public relations articles and history books about the Home and Dr. Sheperd.

Not witnessing the unfolding of their children's accomplishments was a loss for their parents. Had their mother and father been a part of their lives, they would have been proud. Instead, this honor was bestowed on the administrators of Ming Quong and Chung Mei as "substitute parents."

Lonnie lived at Ming Quong before my time. I

knew her later, when I attended the Chinese Presbyterian Church in Oakland's Chinatown. I was in my early teens and living at the Home on Ninth Street. We both sang in the church choir; she sang soprano, and I sang alto. She often sang solos, and I watched anxiously to see if she would hit all the notes with her small frame and deep breaths. She always did, and I could relax!

Lonnie was in her twenties and married to Bob Lee, who also sang in the choir. He was handsome, and I thought he resembled the actor Cary Grant. They had an adorable son, Jeff, whom everyone fussed over. They were one of the pillars of the church, active dedicated members. As Lonnie reflected, "I met Bob at church. We never went out; he just walked me home from church. The church was my second home. I knew nothing else about having a family." The church and the Home were all she knew, although the Home did teach her how to keep house. Was that enough to enter into a marriage? How could the teachers know otherwise? Their lives, too, consisted only of the church and the Home.

Lonnie and Bob lived just a half block from the church in the downstairs flat of a large, two-unit building. By coincidence, my half-sister Ellen lived in the upstairs unit, so I often saw Lonnie's family in passing.

After Lonnie married, she took voice lessons. "There

was so much to learn," she said. "I sang for Eastern Star, weddings, special events, and funerals." At the height of her popularity, owner Charlie Low offered Lonnie a job at his well-known Forbidden City, a San Francisco night-club. People from all over swarmed to this "hot spot," which was known for having the most talented, exotic, and glamorous Chinese women in show business. Lonnie turned him down. "I didn't like that kind of night-club song. That wasn't my life. I like light opera. I sing because I like to sing, not for money."

There had been a handful of MQ girls who were dancers at the club. I wonder whether Donaldina Cameron would have seen the club as an exploiter of Chinese women. These older Ming Quong girls were raised in a strict religious upbringing, but their choice of this profession showed their independent spirit.

Lonnie saw her mother again when she was an adult and sang at a wedding. "I didn't even know she was going to be there," Lonnie told me. "We never talked. I never knew her. But she remarried and kept track of me."

I nodded in response. My next question triggered an unexpected outburst, "How do you feel about everything that's happened to you?" Lonnie got up abruptly, balanced herself on her cane, took a few quick steps away from me, and then suddenly turned to face me. Her eyes were ablaze as she angrily blurted out, "I don't want to talk about it. I felt nothing!" Highly agitated, she repeated what she had said. The last part of her statement, "I felt nothing," stunned me. I wished I could take back that question and avoid what were, obviously, painful feelings. How was one to know that decades later Lonnie's dark memories would trigger such anger? But, after all, I was an MQ girl, and she could take it out on me! Ming Quong girls were used to frankness!

Ironically, I was an adult before I knew Lonnie was a former MQ girl. She never talked about it; the subject just never came up. Other Ming Quong girls who sang in the choir never mentioned that Lonnie was one of us, and Lonnie never attended any of the MQ reunions. Now I understand. Her experience at the Home was not good. She had to rehearse so often instead of playing outside, and she felt Mrs. Chan, a teacher, was "mean." Lonnie recounted one time that Luella painted her nails, which made Mrs. Chan so angry that she put the nail polish on Luella's face, making her face break out.

Lonnie did recall her favorite teacher, Mrs. Lee, with affection: "She was kind." I'm glad Lonnie remembered one good thing about the Home, Mrs. Lee, her role model.

At the one-hundred-twentieth anniversary of the Chinese Presbyterian Church, I was a guest speaker representing Ming Quong. I asked the MQ girls in the audience to come on stage and join in singing the "Lok Hin" song ("We are Little Joy-Givers"), which Mrs. Lee had taught us at the Home. I spotted Lonnie seated next to her husband and in a questioning tone, I said, "Lonnie?" Startled, she looked up at me, then beamed and joined eight of us on stage. Unfortunately, Lonnie and some of the girls in her age group did not know the song. Being a professional, Lonnie scanned the song sheet and quickly started humming. But before she was ready, the piano player began the prelude, and, ready or not, we all attempted to sing. Most of us were off-key, but no one cared. We just continued on and laughed our way through the Lok Hin song. Mrs. Lee would have been so proud of her grown-up MQ girls, especially Lonnie, who had finally returned to the fold.

I asked Lonnie, "Do you have any advice or comments about your life?"

She thought for a few seconds and said, "Well, I guess I had a good life. I'm still married to the same man." Lonnie and Bob have been married over sixty-three years. Bob was a Lincoln School teacher and then an administrator for the Oakland school system. He is an elder at their church. Their married son, Jeff, is an aeronautical engineer and has a daughter.

In conclusion, to pay homage to the "Songbird of Ming Quong," a special haiku for Lonnie:

from the past
a singing voice resonates
forever

14
ONE GIRL, MANY MOTHERS

she spoke no English
her language—everyday love
wrapped in smiles

Everyone at the Oakland Ming Quong buzzed with excitement at that day's coming event—Jean Yee and John Chew were getting married, right there at the Home. John had proposed to her in the Ming Quong library. It seemed only yesterday that Jean, a nondescript refugee, had come to America. Now, there she stood in her white, flowing gown, a beautiful "all-American" bride. The caption of her wedding photo in the Presbyterian Newsletter later read, "Daughter comes home to wed." That Jean had chosen this site had to be a glorious day for the missionary teachers. Jean had been a favorite. She considered each teacher at Ming Quong her surrogate mother and deeply loved each of them. The Home meant the world to Jean. It was truly her haven.

John had lived directly behind Ming Quong in an old Victorian house. He was an easy-going, dependable sort of guy, comfortable to be around and always overlooking the negative things we teen-age girls said and did. The teachers approved of John and allowed us to go on walks with him, which we couldn't do with any other guy. But sometimes Lucianne would take advantage of him and dash off behind his back for the Lincoln School playground. John never mentioned this to the teachers.

Jean's story began in 1946, when, as a tiny, sixteen-year-old, she stepped off the boat from China to America. Her heavy accent and foreign ways led us to assume she had been born in China. In fact, she had lived in the States until age five, but by now memories of what life was like here had faded during the long years in China. She no longer spoke any English. How would she fare at the Oakland Ming Quong Home? The household of thirty teenage girls spoke only limited Cantonese, which, in any event, was not Jean's dialect. Also, the MQ girls' mainstream appearance contrasted sharply with Jean's village attire.

Jean had experienced a horrific time in China, so

when she arrived at Ming Quong, she appreciated everything. This trait helped bridge her way over the hurdles.

Living with a girl who could not comprehend anything was different. Normally, we gathered around a newcomer, glanced at her belongings while she unpacked, and welcomed her with questions about her family, her age, and where she came from. But all Jean could do was smile, which at least told us she was nice.

The teachers maintained a code of silence about everyone's past, which was pure frustration for us. Now came Jean, who was quite grown up and could have related her history—but she couldn't tell us a thing! Fortunately, some new girls who could speak Jean's dialect arrived later. Jean was actually glad that the household spoke only English. She picked it up quickly. In fact, she was way ahead of her public school friends who only spoke Chinese at home.

A group of us American-born girls often huddled together, giggling silently outside Jean's closed bedroom door to listen to screechy, high-pitched wailing sounds coming from within. Although it sounded like someone in pain, we knew it was only Jean and her sister Katie. We covered our mouths to stifle our laughter, realizing all the while how truly obnoxious we were, but we couldn't help ourselves. Never before had we heard such sounds.

Standing outside their door, I could easily imagine a sparse theatrical stage and heavily made-up, costumed sisters with threatening expressions!

But now, I appreciate the sisters' theatrical renderings. They did sound just like those classic Chinese movies that I've seen later in life. In essence, they had actually captured the culture and provided us with our first musical sounds of China.

Jean had an unbelievably kind spirit, something we didn't recognize at the time. Most of us thought she was too "goody-goody," too "Chinese-y," and not at all "Americanized." All the MQ teachers gravitated to Jean, however. She had the innocence of a young child—open, loving, helpful, obedient, and eager to learn. She was any parent's dream, especially for the missionary teachers, who could now nurture a loving daughter.

The rest of us thought the teachers favored Jean and her older sister, Katie. Jean and Katie were allowed to sleep downstairs in a wing far away from any of the teachers' bedrooms. Wasn't that favoritism? We thought they got this privilege because they always volunteered for chores they didn't really have to do. Even though Jean was not assigned kitchen duties, she was there each day, working and setting the dining room tables at every mealtime.

But, in reality, the extra work and sleeping privilege

only happened because of Jean's unusual circumstances, which I learned about years later:

Jean's mother died when Jean was five. Even though her father had heard of Ming Quong, he did not want to separate his family of six children. He decided to take everyone back to China. While there, he remarried, but he later returned to America to work, leaving his children with their stepmother. Life changed drastically for the family remaining in China. The Japanese and Chinese were at war, and Jean's village was caught in the crossfire. "Bullets and bombs were flying and bursting all around us. Japanese soldiers were raiding villages. I starved. I had limited clothing and no shoes. My family was almost penniless." During her ten-year stay in China, Jean was able to attend school for only four-and-a-half years. "I was stranded in China because of World War II," Jean said, "It was an intense childhood, but I still experienced happiness, because I didn't know any other way of life."

Jean's oldest sister, Helen, lived with her husband and baby just around the corner from Ming Quong. Jean and Katie slept at Ming Quong, but they otherwise stayed and ate at Helen's house. Since they only needed lodging, Ming Quong only charged the two girls fifteen dollars a month, paid by their father, who had now gone back to China.

However, Helen and her husband worked different shifts, and the husband slept during the day. Jean and Katie did not want to disturb his sleep and went without breakfast or lunch, surviving only on cookies at school. When Miss Higgins realized that the girls weren't eating, she offered them three meals a day at MQ, but they were to do a daily hour-and-a-half of extra chores in exchange. Jean and Katie became assistants to the cook and helped in the dining room. There was also one more important requirement: they had to obey all the rules of the Home, just like the other MQ girls, even though they were only lodgers. "Rules!" Jean was delighted. "I thought rules meant caring. I grew up with no one who cared what I did or where I was. I valued the rules more than the meals. My stepmother, with whom I lived in China after my father came to America, was a nice person, but I was always searching for more—for love and approval." In Jean's words, she had "found heaven's gate." She now felt safe and secure, with food and second-hand clothing from the church. And she had an extended family. "At first, I was overwhelmed by the teachers' warmth and didn't know how to react. Because I could not speak English, I smiled a lot, and soon my smiles became love."

And now I knew why Jean and her sister slept downstairs—not because they were privileged girls, but because they had so much work and homework to do. But, of course, they were well-behaved sisters and could be trusted!

One night when we were in our sixties and seventies, a group of MQ girls actually had a real "slumber party" at Jean's home! First we attended an intriguing concert by a young African-American Oakland boy who sang American hymns in Chinese by memorizing the Chinese sounds. Later, at Jean's house, while the rest of us were immersed in conversation, Jean slipped out to the kitchen, and soon an aromatic fragrance of smoked turkey legs, fresh ginger, and rice drifted into the living room. She was making *jook* for our breakfast! This brew simmered slowly all night in a giant cooking pot. This fun memory is forever forged in my mind.

The next morning, we attended the small Chinese church where Jean's family were active members. The atmosphere was intimate, with emphasis on the individual, quite different from the traditional Chinese Presbyterian Church we had all attended while at the Home.

Jean's memories of the Home are always positive, except for one troubling aspect, which makes her eyes well up with tears. "When the girls turned sixteen, they had to leave the Home and work for a family. There was no follow-up with the girls after they left Ming Quong.

On their days off, they had nowhere to go and often just ended up sitting alone on a bench with nothing to eat except some crackers. Jean saw the loneliness of these girls and worried about what would happen to her when she had to leave. Where would she live? How would she get her next meal? Nightmares followed. Anxiety ridden, she accepted what life presented to her—John's proposal of marriage. "I was fortunate," Jean said. "John was a wonderful person and a Christian."

Today, Jean is the mother of three daughters and the grandmother of two grandchildren. A wonderful watercolorist, she writes and illustrates children's books. She volunteers at the Chabot Observatory in Oakland and helps the homeless by distributing clothing, blankets, and sundries.

As adults, Jean and I are good friends. She and John have attended almost all of my book readings, each time bringing roses and special gifts!

Jean always remained a caring daughter to the Ming Quong teachers. She wrote letters, sent Mother's Day cards, saw them at church, visited them later at their retirement homes. Once, a group of us MQ women went with Jean to see a former teacher, Miss Davies, at her retirement home. We arranged a well-received special program to tell the residents about her work at Ming

Quong. Back at Miss Davies' apartment, I overheard Jean's daughters calling Miss Davies, "Grandma." It seemed Jean's children had as many grandmothers as Jean had mothers!

15

THE LOTUS

feisty Chinese girl
in a black neighborhood
muscles like Popeye!

From the depths of the murkiest, poorest ghetto in San Francisco's Bayview-Hunter's Point neighborhood, a tough tomboy emerged. This homely, buck-toothed eleven-year-old girl, Janet Chang, was already feared in her tough neighborhood of predominately African-American neighbors. A chronic troublemaker, she was suspended from school many times for fights. Janet was an embarrassment to her harried mother, who was raising five children alone. With no one around to help her, Janet's mother turned to Donaldina Cameron, who recommended that Janet be placed at the Ming Quong Home in Los Gatos.

Janet came to the Home during a transitional period in 1959, long after I had left.

The new, homey atmosphere and relaxed environment would seem to have been the perfect place for a young girl from the ghetto to live, safe and free from everyday tensions and fights. Janet did not see it that way, however. She stated, "As my mother packed my clothes in a cardboard box, she mumbled something about sending me to camp. After the long drive from San Francisco, we drove through a tall, wooden gate with a sign that read, 'Ming Quong Home.' I knew immediately that this was not a camp with horses, a lake, or campfires with marshmallows. My mother dropped me off without explanation or a good-bye.

"My first day, someone told me to go out and play with the other girls. Confused and lacking social skills, I immediately engaged in a physical fight. After leaving my opponent bruised, dirty, and on the ground, I re-entered the cottage and headed straight to my room.

"The housemother, Miss Martin, walked towards me, backlit by the rear window. She was extremely ugly. With thick glasses over unkind eyes, her jowls dropping to her chest, her pendulous breasts hanging over her belt, and her belly falling over her knees, she eyed me as her target. She had her arms behind her back, hiding something. As she lurched closer, she revealed a hairbrush as her weapon and moved to hit me. I countered her swing, stared deliberately into her eyes, and said, 'No one spanks or hits me. If you touch me, I will return twice the power and hurt you. I will go to my room. I will not attend dinner. I will not come out until the morning.' No one ever laid a hand on me during my stay."

I first met Janet, not at the Home, but at one of my book readings. She had been way in the back of the large, crowded, library room, yet she dodged all the people in front of her to be first one in line to talk to me. In a matter of seconds, this intense woman rattled off her own experiences at the Home, thanked me for coming, mumbled something about having to be someplace, and, just like that, was gone.

Sometime later I saw her again at a mutual friend's birthday celebration. She stood out like a fairy-tale princess, shining brightly in a room of over two hundred other smartly dressed, high-society women. She seemed to be at home in all that elegance. She smiled broadly as she eagerly introduced me to her equally handsome escort, and I thought to myself, what a nice-looking couple.

How did all this happen, given her less-than-stellar origins? Like a beautiful lotus, she had emerged from her dark beginnings. The answer was to be found in her experiences at the Home!

Ming Quong after my time had many resources available to the girls. Many specialists volunteered their services, and the girls were often tested on reading, writing, and IQ. To Janet's benefit, she was teamed up with an insightful person who opened her eyes to another type of life. One day while waiting on the front steps of the main house, a cool sports car came cruising up the driveway, looped around the large flower bed, and stopped in front of her. The door opened and out stepped a red-haired lady with freckles who acknowledged Janet with a smile. Janet felt like a character in a fantasy. The most unforgettable part of this encounter was the human connection, the woman's smile. No one had ever greeted her like that.

Each testing day, Janet looked forward to the lady's smile. The two were a team, sitting for hours at the library as Janet answered all the test questions without hesitation. Janet scored high on the exams. To her surprise, she learned an important factor about herself—she was smart!

After living over two years at Ming Quong, she returned home to San Francisco full of confidence. However, she was confronted at school by the usual bullies who did not want a "chink" around. Once again, Janet's survival instincts surfaced, and her powerful fist and repertoire of threats squashed the bullies. While she survived that particular incident, she wanted out of that environment. Remembering the red-haired lady's comments that she was smart, she knew she had the ability to achieve what she wanted. Armed with her fierce spirit, she set out to attend the most prestigious school in San Francisco: Lowell College Preparatory High School. Her first request was denied, but she persevered and requested the test scores from the red-haired lady. Finally, Janet was accepted at Lowell.

She eventually became a registered nurse with a B.S. and a Master's in public health. Today she is the Director of Student Health Services at San Jose State College. In addition, she instructs health education classes at the University of California at Santa Cruz, San Jose City College, and National University.

In Janet's words, she had not only achieved the American dream, but "surpassed it, moving among the top one percent economically in our country, living in a nice home in the nicest neighborhood, driving a Mercedes-Benz, travelling, going on cruises with my family, and belonging to the most exclusive tennis club in the area. By outward appearances, no one could tell I was once a juvenile delinquent."

Janet volunteers for worthy causes. Every year she finds an organization and pitches in, spearheading the effort for coats for kids, purses for the poor, and suitcases for the homeless. Wherever Janet is, you can bet she's in there smiling and giving her best.

Grateful for her time at Ming Quong, she credits the Home for redirecting her life from the chaos of anti-social behavior and giving her another chance in life.

16

THE SUMMER GIRL

ambitious girl
her legacy
mother to all

One morning the phone rang at the back of my store while I was redecorating the front window. Trapped in a tight area, I moved as quickly as I could to maneuver my now-stiffened body out of the small area without bumping into any merchandise. I barely made it to the phone before the answering machine kicked in.

"Hey, what took you so long?" laughed Rhoda from the other end of the line. "I've got news for you!" she added excitedly. "Bea Wong's been named Mother of the Year for Oakland!"

This happened in 2006. What an honor for a friend, and her being a former Ming Quong girl made it all the sweeter.

Beatrice Lee (Wong) came to the Los Gatos home at the age of ten because she had asthma and her mother had died. For the first two years, she was a "summer girl," staying at the Home for her health. Later, she returned for full-time residency.

We girls never knew who paid for our living expenses at Ming Quong. We just lived there, bonded by a common need. However, the historical ledger showed how each girl's expenses were met. While the government supported many of the girls at Ming Quong, Bea's stay was paid for by her father, a fact of which she was most proud, as she had not been "on welfare." As an adult, she rarely mentioned her life at Ming Quong to friends or associates.

Bea's father figured into the life of every Ming Quong girl in one way that remains a sweet memory for me. He visited monthly and came during the hot days of summer bearing something he instinctively knew his daughter and her new friends would like—the biggest, juiciest watermelons he could find. Watermelon was not on our institutional menu, so sharing in this largesse was one of the highlights of summer. Cheerful sounds reverberated around the dining room as we enjoyed our first bite. The sweet fruit was mouth-watering and so flavorful. We spooned each precious piece down to the forbidden white rind. We sighed, wishing for one more red bite, but there were never seconds.

After each sweet treat, Miss Bankes, the Head of the Home, tapped her water-glass for an important announcement. We always knew what she was going to say, but we listened attentively anyway as she announced that our watermelon dessert was a gift from Bea's father. All heads turned towards Bea's table. Her twinkling eyes and proud smile were all a father could wish to see. His heart would have melted. We adored Bea because of her father's generosity.

She told me years later that her father had also helped hang the majestic Chinese sign at the Home. The gentle curve of the expansive sign always reminded me of a giant, winged bird in flight. I had often stood beneath the sign, feeling small next to its height.

Asked for her significant memories of Ming Quong, Bea smiled and mentioned her lifelong friends, like Pansy and Rhoda. "It was just the right chemistry; it just worked." Then she added sadly, "Nona, I always felt sorry for you because you ate so slowly. You were always the last one to leave the dining room, and when they turned off the lights, you had to sit in the dark for hours until you finished your meal." It was true! We were not allowed to waste food at Ming Quong.

Bea and her husband, George, owned two family-operated grocery stores in Oakland and Richmond and have two daughters and four grandsons. Despite the demands of work and family, she has worked tirelessly for decades to help others.

Her dedication was acknowledged in 2006 by the City of Oakland when Bea was named "Mother of the Year." The nomination board said of her, "She embodies the spirit of what we define as a 'Mother.' Mrs. Wong has been a dedicated humanitarian who never asks for anything in return from the people she loves to serve ..." Now in her eighties, Bea still garners awards, the last in 2010 for her volunteer activities with the Friends of the Asian Library in Oakland's Chinatown.

Bea's many charitable activities are too numerous to list fully. She and eleven colleagues founded the Oakland Chinese Chamber of Commerce. She is well-known for selling raffle tickets to "everyone." One year, she alone raised ten thousand dollars for Oakland Chinatown's Lion's Club. She worked with immigrants adjusting to life in America, assuaging their fears and giving them direction so that no one felt alone or bewildered.

As adults, Bea and I belonged to the Chinese Women's Society in Oakland. I saw first-hand how she worked, diligently getting things done with no fooling around.

For example, I once volunteered to pass out flyers at the Chinese Chamber of Commerce booth at the Chinatown Street Festival and was having fun chatting with hundreds of passers-by and friends. To my surprise, Bea admonished me! I was talking too much and not doing my job! That directness is a characteristic of MQ girls: We generally say what we mean, with no hard feelings.

Bea and George reside only two blocks from my half-sister, Ellen, in Oakland, in an area known as "China Hill." When I visited Ellen, I often also dropped in to see Bea without any prior notice. She always greeted me with a cheerful smile. Her home was inviting, displaying interesting Chinese artifacts, plaques, awards, family pictures, and a life-size, color photo of her beautiful oldest daughter, Sandy, who was Miss Chinatown USA in 1973.

Bea's long, hard journey has certainly benefited the Oakland community. She takes pride in passing down to her daughters and grandsons the values of volunteerism and generosity, initially instilled in her by her father. Her daughter, Karen, especially, is active in the Oakland Chinatown community. A plaque commemorating Bea as Mother-of-the-Year was placed in Oakland's Rose Garden, where you will also see the names of two other Mothers-of-the-Year connected with Ming Quong: Mrs.

Carol Martin, a former MQ teacher, and my aunt, Mrs. Cecilia Ho, who volunteered countless hours at Lincoln Elementary where we attended school. They all exemplify the spiritual meaning of Ming Quong: "Radiant Light."

17

LITTLE BABY-BYE

Little Baby-Bye
Ming Quong's oldest senior girl
singing all through life

Helen Mae Wong (Kee) had the distinction of being the oldest former Ming Quong girl around. She was ninety-three in 2000, the year in which I interviewed her. I knew her well and sometimes kidded her by saying, "Here we are—the youngest and the oldest" (at one time I was the youngest). Helen always giggled with delight. Every time I saw her, I was amazed at her vibrant persona and her meticulous and glamorous appearance, complete with bright-red nail polish and matching lipstick.

At the Home, "Baby-Bye" was Helen's nickname because that was the name of her favorite song. One could hear her humming or singing it all day:

Baby-Bye shut your little eye
Go to sleep

. . .

I say good-bye to you.

My Aunt Yet, who lived with Helen at the Ming Quong Home next to Mills College, said Helen was also nicknamed "China Doll" because she was so tiny and fragile, with the traditional rice bowl haircut and straight bangs.

Helen's mother was a "picture bride" (a woman photographed for a book that single men used to select a bride from afar). She married an older man in America and had Helen and another daughter. This man also had a wife in China. When he asked Helen's mother to return to China with him, she refused, having no desire to be his second wife there. So Helen's mother stayed in America and remarried. Her two very young daughters did not fit into her new life, so she left two-and-a-half-year-old Helen and her five-and-a-half-year-old sister at their half-brother's place in San Francisco Chinatown. Unfortunately, this half-brother was a shady character who not only ran the gambling joints in Chinatown but had a wife who was a prostitute.

When Donaldina Cameron became aware of this

situation, she immediately intervened and brought the two sisters to the rescue mission "920" in San Francisco. Soon it became too crowded there, and the two sisters went to another home, the Tooker Home in Oakland. Every Sunday at the Tooker Home, the girls were dressed in two-piece Chinese outfits and walked two-by-two to the Oakland Chinese Presbyterian Church on Eighth Street.

When she lived at the Ming Quong Home near Mills, Helen's half-brother came to visit and always brought delectable food because Helen and her sister had told him they didn't care for the Home's food. One of the favorites he brought was lop cheung, or Chinese sausage. All the other girls wanted to sit at Helen's table for dinner on those nights, but that was impossible, as each girl was assigned to a particular table with a teacher.

Helen happened to be related to the teacher, Mrs. Linn (also known as Mrs. Lee), so she and her sister called her "Auntie." Helen remembered with great admiration that her auntie never had a bad word for anyone.

Helen also fondly remembers that Miss Mills (no relation to Mills College), a teacher who favored her, would take Helen into her bedroom, give her candy, and tell her to keep it a secret.

Helen smiled when telling me about Miss Mills, but

her smile faded as she recalled a different, vivid memory that made her angry and sad at the same time. She said that her roommate wet her bed so often that the teachers feared the girl's bedsprings would rust, so they forced her to sleep on a board.

The teachers never told the girls about the facts of life. They learned from each other. When they started to menstruate, they kept it to themselves, too embarrassed to tell anyone. No one talked about boys and dating, but later Helen was always at ease when she dated.

After graduating from Oakland High School, Helen worked for a Caucasian couple in exchange for room and board. The husband was a doctor. One time when his wife was back east, the doctor wanted her to go to bed with him. Terrified, Helen called Miss Mills immediately, and Helen went back to live with her half-brother in San Francisco Chinatown. By then, Helen was old enough not to be influenced by her brother's lifestyle.

Helen attended San Francisco State University, studying to become a teacher. When she applied for a secretarial job at the National Dollar Store on Fillmore Street in San Francisco, Bill Kee, the assistant manager, hired her immediately. He liked her and said, "This is the girl I'm going to marry"! The manager of the store also liked Helen, but he already had a wife in China, so Helen dated Bill. When he proposed, she refused him, with the statement, "You're just an assistant manager. When you become the manager, I will marry you!" Two months later, he did get promoted, and they were wed.

Once an active member of the Oakland Chinese Presbyterian Church, Helen later left Oakland for the On Lok senior home in San Francisco Chinatown. While in Oakland, she was very supportive and generous with her donations in restoring the church, including two beautiful, stained-glass doors for the front entrance. Every week at the church's senior program, she led the seniors into singing joyfully and with great energy, as she had sung as a child. She definitely woke up the ladies! Because the church was located one block from busy Chinatown, there was no parking nearby, except the handicapped space right in front. Guess who got to park there as a sign of how much the church respected her? The one and only Helen Kee!

Oakland Mayor Lionel Wilson appointed Helen in her early 80s to the Commission of the Aging, a position which she held for ten years. She was also on the advisory councils for all Oakland's senior centers for twenty years.

During the low time in her life after her husband, Bill, passed away, she mentioned how her two daughters and their families were very supportive. She talked fondly about her family and reminded me that her oldest daughter, Gerrye Wong, was a former teacher and a writer/columnist for San Francisco *Asian Week*.

At the end of our interview, Helen's last words were, "My life was blessed."

My memories of Helen are vivid. I knew her in church and saw her on many occasions. In Oakland, she lived just a few blocks from my half-sister, Ellen. Sometimes while visiting my sister, I would walk over to Helen's house, which had zillions of steep stairs. How Helen climbed those stairs year after year, I'll never know. She never got winded, but I was out of breath! I'm sure that managing those stairs kept her young.

Helen's home was filled with miniature Chinese artifacts in ivory, jade, and soapstone, many of museum quality. Outside on her covered patio, she had the largest collection of orchids I had ever seen in a private residence. Many were set up on tables, where they dwarfed Helen. That didn't bother her, however. Whenever she needed a sprig of orchid for a friend or the church, she just had her giant of a husband clip them! Every Mother's Day, Helen presented an orchid corsage for each mother in attendance at church.

Helen loved food. She always ate more than I did and never gained an ounce! A terrific cook, she made the best sticky rice with Chinese sausage, dried shrimp, salted eggs, and minced dried mushrooms steamed in tea leaves. It was heavenly. And for sweets, she was famous for her homemade coffee candy.

I felt blessed by Helen's grand presence. The oldest and the youngest, we were a good pair, and, like Mutt and Jeff, we were also the tallest and the shortest!

THE A'S FAN

annoyed— she moves on
aggravation not worth it
just choose your own path

"Take me out to the ball game; take me out with the crowd ..." The familiar baseball song strums in your head as you weave your way among seated sports fans, trying to avoid their jutting kneecaps and stepping over out-stretched feet to get to your assigned seat. You spot it and settle down for a long day of exhilarated cheering with other fans. But let's hope you're in the correct seat, or you just might hear a booming voice directed towards you: "Let me see your ticket. You don't belong here. Go up to the next level." This command would not be what you'd expect from the typical, quiet Asian woman, but it would be Ethel Yee (Wong), a tiny, former Ming Quong girl who does not fit the stereotype. She has been an usher for the Oakland A's baseball team for close to twenty years. As the oldest of her co-workers, she knows the nuances of her job. No one can pull a fast one on her. She loves her work and has always acknowledged the regular fans with her friendly smile.

That's Ethel, a plain, no-nonsense girl, who at the Home never fussed or bothered about her appearance. What she cared about was sports. She came to the Home in Los Gatos (rather than the Oakland Home) when she was in high school in order to keep her together with her two younger sisters, Emily and Gloria. Being an outgoing person, she mingled easily with students who were sports enthusiasts and athletes.

Ethel and her sisters were from Salinas, California, where their father was a gambler. They lived with him and an uncle after their mother died. When their father also died, they were sent to the Home. In those days, girls did not live alone with an uncle. There was one other older Ming Quong girl who had also been separated from her uncle under similar circumstances, and that caused her much pain. Ethel did not express similar regrets. I surmised that even in her pre-adolescent years, Ethel's philosophy was just to face the facts and move on.

Ethel and I lived at the Los Gatos Ming Quong Home at the same time. She was eight years older, so we hardly knew each other back then, although we "clicked" after meeting again as adults. Even though we girls were raised together, we often didn't know each other well, especially if we were not in the same age group. But sharing the special status as residents of the Home bonded us in itself. For me, writing this book and learning about the girls' lives before and after leaving Ming Quong was like forming new friendships. Sometimes I would be surprised by or in awe of their experiences and thought to myself that this was once the girl I grew up with at the Home! I would smile and get a good feeling deep within. I'm sure some of the Ming Quong teachers experienced a similar satisfaction as their birds flew the nest, like parents in a "real" family!

Although Ethel was an independent individual set in her ways when she came to Ming Quong, her flexible outlook on life helped her adjust easily to a large household of different personalities and strict teachers with stringent rules. She added that if you didn't get along with your family, there were plenty of girls at the Home to have as friends. Ethel never detailed her past experiences to me, but the way she viewed life, there was no need to.

Ethel often took BART (the Bay Area Rapid Transit system: the metro railway in the San Francisco Bay Area) from her home in Oakland Chinatown to visit me at my store in Walnut Creek. She once gave me a handmade, Christmas-angel ornament made of soft felt. It was really nice to see her creative side. Until then, I had only known about her love for sports.

After high school, it was time for Ethel to leave the Home, but she had nowhere to go. Her rapport with the teachers made it possible for her to live temporarily in the downstairs wing of the Oakland Ming Quong Home, which was usually reserved for "other," non-Ming-Quong girls. She paid twenty-five dollars a month for room and board until she figured out her future plans.

The Home eventually found her a live-in job in Piedmont caring for a baby and a preschooler. Meanwhile, she also got employment as a clerk-typist at the Oakland Naval Supply Center. After two months of juggling two jobs, she quit her house-job and moved in with two other MQ girls, Bernice and Florence Lee, at their father's home. Now Ethel was on her own and, with her spirit, she was destined to do well.

Ethel met her husband, George Wong, an auto-mechanic, at a Chinese folk dance group at the YMCA in San Francisco. He was handsome, unassuming, and quiet, the opposite of Ethel! They made a good pair.

George and Ethel both attended the Chinese Presbyterian Church on Eighth Street in Oakland, where their relationship blossomed. This was the church the Ming Quong girls attended every Sunday. The minister, Mok See, was very kind and gentle. After each church service, the congregation lined up to shake his hand. He always smiled tenderly, and his twinkling eyes conveyed his enveloping love. Even though I did not understand his long sermons in Chinese and unfavorably compared this very old-looking church to the modern one we had attended in Los Gatos, the genuineness of Mok See made it all worthwhile!

George and Ethel were married at this church. By coincidence, another Ming Quong girl, Bessie (Boots) and Dave Aoki were also to be married by Mok See on the same day in the same church. That was advantageous for both couples, as their economical upbringing at the Home surfaced, and they realized they could save money by using the same flowers at the church! Ethel was married first, so Boots kept the flowers for her wedding and reception at the church's social hall. The disappointing side of this was that some girls were unable to attend both weddings. "Not many MQ gals came to my wedding," Ethel remarked. "Even Rhoda couldn't come, because she was in Boots's wedding!"

But there was an interesting twist: Because Boots's

reception was scheduled for the church, Ethel had to find another location for hers. She remembered that some older girls had used the Ninth Street Home for their receptions, and that was where she held hers. She was once again back at Ming Quong. The interior featured dark, rich wood, shiny hardwood floors, and classic light fixtures, all flanked by an elegant, curved staircase. Classic Chinese carved furniture accented the luxurious oriental rugs.

Ethel and George had a daughter and son. Just two months short of working at Naval Supply Center for ten years, Ethel quit to become a full-time mother. Behind this decision was her mother-in-law, who had ten children and told Ethel, "You should stay home and take care of your children." That surprised me, as I always thought Ethel would be out in the work force and not a homemaker. George's mother's heartfelt advice worked. As Emily, Ethel's sister, said, "Ethel's children turned out well."

Ethel's later life was full of activities involving sports. She competed in bowling tournaments and was secretary of the Chinese League Bowling Club for twenty-nine years. And she rewarded any player who scored low with one of her handmade stuffed animals! She is now in her eighties and looks twenty years younger!

In 1999, after about six years had passed since the prior MQ reunion, Ethel and I decided it was time for another one. That's how our reunions came about: Whoever felt the urge to do one just did it. Everything fell into place. We did all the planning casually at my store. We kept it simple, reasonable, and easy. Our foremost thought was, where should it take place? MQ, of course! Right away we secured Alderwood Hall, the former Ming Quong Home that was now part of Mills College. Tommiette Reys, a great Ming Quong friend, was the director there, and she offered the place to us completely free of charge! When we spoke of food, she even arranged for Mills to cater the affair at an affordable price and added a free gourmet salad to the buffet! The food was divine, and the price was perfect. From the admission fees, we paid for everything and had enough left over for a gift for Tommiette, donations to Mills College and Eastfield Ming Quong (Ming Quong had since merged with another orphanage) and seed money for anyone who wanted to plan another reunion!

Over sixty people attended. For the first time at any reunion, we had invited a group of very special guests, the former residents of the Chung Mei Home for boys. Six of them came, some with wives and some alone. A handsome Chung Mei man named Ron attended with his two MQ sisters, Edna and Nora. They told him to "go in there and meet some girls." Ron, not being shy, waltzed right in and found the perfect girl! Like a magnet he approached a petite, friendly woman and lavished his attentions on her. He, of course, didn't know she was a happily married woman with three daughters and two grandchildren—our very own MQ girl, Jean Yee Chew! She, of course, smiled a lot! Surprised and flattered, she looked radiant.

At the day's end, Helen Wong, who was in her eighties and had been one of the original girls living on the premises, was also smiling. She said, "This reunion was the most fun, better than the last one!" That was a rare compliment coming from an astute woman who was always very serious. Our sides ached from all the laughter and good cheer. What made it more memorable was that this successful event had all been planned with ease at my Ming Quong store! What fun!

Here are some of Ethel's musings on life:

"I've been very fortunate and lucky."

"We can't choose our parents, but we can choose our friends."

"Don't make enemies, just walk on by."

"My happiest time was at Ming Quong."

Now, please remember this about Ethel: If you attend an Oakland's A's baseball game, sit in the seat assigned to you, or, there's a good possibility a spirited, petite grandmother of six will holler at you!

19
JOYFUL, JOYFUL, WE ADORE THEE

assassinated
in China life was cheap
daughter carries on

What's in a name? Everything, as in the case of Ruth Joy Wu (Wong). Joy is her middle name, and that is what she was, an absolute joy. Her parents had given her the perfect name, and she completely lived it. At Ming Quong, she portrayed a joyful spirit, always helpful, gracious, and kind. In her age group, of which she was one of the oldest, the girls and even the teachers called her "Joy." My Nursery group, the youngest ones, called her Ruth Joy.

As recorded in the Ming Quong ledger, seven-year-old Ruth Joy came to the Home from Indiana in 1931 as a "deserted child" in need of "Chinese associates." Given her abandonment in life, her joyfulness was remarkable.

Ruth Joy was born during China's political upheaval when life was chaotic and unpredictable. She told me: "My father joined the Sun Yat-sen Revolution and was assassinated by the warlords shortly after my birth. He and two other university students had gone to one of the warlords to make peace, believing that he was sympathetic to their cause. In fact, all three were assassinated. Life was so cheap in China during those days. My father was supposed to join my mother in America, but that never happened."

Ruth Joy's strong spirit carried her through her childhood. She lived at all three of the Ming Quong Homes. She stayed at the Los Gatos Home for many years, even after the other girls in her age group had moved to the Oakland home on Ninth Street, because she was needed to assist Miss Chew with the Nursery group.

"I used to help Hung Mui (Miss Chew) care for the younger children. I would get them up in the morning and dress and comb their hair before they took off for school. This included you, Nona. You were the youngest ever admitted to the Home." That Ruth Joy remembered me made me feel special, as I cherished her gentle ways. We were fortunate she was Miss Chew's helper.

Ruth Joy became one of the first girls to live at Ming Quong, and for the teachers, raising orphans and needy children was a vast undertaking. Everything was a learning experience. When reading *Chopstick Childhood,* Ruth Joy was surprised to learn how some of the teachers had treated the girls. "I really do not recall any negative experiences while I was there. I remember Miss Higgins was very good to me."

Nevertheless, many rules existed, and if they were broken, punishment followed. Once a young, "well-behaved" girl stole a barrette, and her punishment was being placed in a cage! We all thought that was harsh, or, as we called it back then, "mean." In truth, some teachers *were* just plain mean, while others were very nice. What made us sad was that most of the nice ones never stayed.

The cage incident and other punishments happened after Ruth Joy left the Home. She left Ming Quong in 1939 when she graduated from Los Gatos High School. Her departure was felt by all.

Throughout the years I often heard the older girls talk about Ruth Joy. They were proud of her accomplishments. Her resume would dazzle a Christmas tree!

She graduated from the University of California, San Francisco (UCSF) School of Nursing in 1946 but never practiced as a nurse. She earned her Master's degree from New York University and Wayne State University in Detroit. She subsequently earned a Ph.D. in education at UCLA. From 1972 to 1982, she was Chair for the Department of Nursing at her alma mater, during which time she wrote *Behavior and Illness,* published by Prentice-Hall. This book was used primarily by nursing schools as a text.

In 1982 she became Acting Associate Dean, then Acting Dean at UCSF School of Nursing for one year. Her last job began in 1984 as a Dean for the California State University of Los Angeles, School of Health and Human Services. She retired in 1995.

What an intellect! She had enough education, degrees, and different jobs for everyone in her age group! I am astounded, almost speechless, at her accomplishments—I am a writer without words! But I can't be a writer without words because there is more to write!

In her personal life, Ruth Joy married in 1951 and had two sons, Randy and James, and five grandchildren. She is now a great-grandmother. Her husband died in 2002. At one point, she reflected back to her childhood and said, "I am really thankful that my mother never took me back to China." She added, "I have met my mother and father's families, which include several cousins living in the U.S."

What a full life. The Ming Quong teachers would-have been overwhelmed and overjoyed at her achievements. They would have beamed proudly, remembering the quiet and helpful seven-year-old when she came to the Home.

One teacher in particular, Mrs. Linn (Lee), would have been the proudest one of all, for Joy was like a "daughter" to her later in life. Ruth Joy developed a close relationship with Mrs. Linn at the Home, and it grew stronger later, after the death of Mrs. Linn's daughter, Mildred, who was Ruth Joy's close friend. Ruth Joy visited Mrs. Linn frequently, and, as Ruth Joy said, "She became like a mother to me." In the end, when Mrs. Linn passed on, Ruth Joy became the hostess to the MQ girls who traveled to the Los Angeles area for her memorial service. Once again, with joyfulness, Ruth Joy took care of her Ming Quong siblings.

20 FULL OF SURPRISES

one never knows
what this outspoken girl
will say or do

Quick-witted Bernice Wong stands out in my mind as being quite bold and mischievous.

During summer vacation at the Los Gatos Home, we older girls worked by cutting apricots and picking prunes. After the working season, we usually celebrated by putting on impromptu plays at the old barn, which was perfect for a makeshift stage. Anyone who wanted to create a skit dolled up in unusual clothing. Once some girls even borrowed garments from an easy-going teacher, Miss Bergman.

Bernice had a rather bony frame and had the mannerisms of a foreign-born girl. When she came on stage dressed like the popular movie star, Carmen Miranda, everyone was enthused. She resembled the flashy singing star with her glamorous smile. Bernice twirled her scarves and bellowed crazy tunes, prancing and dancing rather awkwardly, but with oomph. Oh, did we laugh, including the surprised teacher, who just happened to attend the skits that day. Suddenly, Bernice stopped and, with her back to us, she bent over and flipped up her ruffled skirt to bare colorful bloomers! That was Bernice, full of surprises!

Now here is Bernice's story. In sharing it, she revealed more wonderful surprises.

Bernice came by ship with her brother, Wayne, two cousins, and father from Hong Kong in 1940 to live with relatives in San Francisco. Her mother stayed behind in Hong Kong. At first, Bernice and Wayne received no education in California. Her father worked every day and could not take care of them. They later attended the Commodore Elementary School in Chinatown, where they were frightened, as their relatives had not prepared them for what to expect at school.

Bernice's father had heard about Donaldina Cameron and contacted the Mission. Lorna Logan (successor to Donaldina Cameron) suggested Bernice go to the Los Gatos Home, and she stayed from 1941 to 1945. She then transferred to the Oakland Home. Her brother, Wayne, went to Chung Mei.

While she was in ninth grade at Oakland Technical High School, Bernice's father moved her back from Ming Quong to San Francisco, where she graduated from Galileo High. Wayne also moved back from Chung Mei and lived with their father for a while.

She remembers a special evening at the Los Gatos Home. She had asked Miss Hayes, if she could invite her teacher from school, Mrs. Teal, to have dinner with her at the Home. Miss Hayes decided to invite all the girls' teachers to come. Mrs. Lee, our Chinese School teacher at MQ who occasionally made Chinese food for us, cooked Chinese dinner—tomato beef over rice—and for dessert, they had sliced oranges. After dinner, they all went upstairs to the living room for vespers, and the music teacher from the school played the piano. They all had an enjoyable time singing songs.

I recalled how my classmates had always wanted to come up to the Home for dinner, but that never happened. To hear that Bernice had actually accomplished having all those dinner guests was a pleasant surprise. I wish I could have been there. She was a girl with a lot of gumption.

One Christmas at the Oakland Home, a few of the MQ girls—Carol, Amy, Paula, and Bernice—were ballet dancers for a pageant at the Oakland Auditorium. That's another event I wish I could have attended. MQ girls as ballerinas—that was a fun surprise!

Bernice wrote a winning poem about safety in everyday living for the Latham Foundation contest. She won a twenty-five-dollar U.S. war bond and appeared on a radio broadcast at the Oakland Tribune with three other students. Because Bernice was terribly scared, Miss Musgrave, successor to Miss Higgins, made her practice reading it out loud many times and accompanied her to the broadcast. It was wonderful to hear about Miss Musgrave encouraging Bernice to write poetry, as she had encouraged me to play an angel in the Christmas play. A teacher of the arts! As Bernice said, "Ming Quong was the happiest time of my life."

Bernice did feel, however, that the teachers at the Homes failed at one thing. The lack of family planning education left the girls unprepared for marriage and the real world. She feels that's why, like her, a lot of the girls divorced and raised their children as single parents.

An unforgettable memory of Bernice happened when she and I attended Bingo's memorial service in 1998 at the San Francisco Art Institute. As one of the speakers, I shared about Bingo's life at Ming Quong, which surprised many attendees who were not aware that she had lived at MQ. Many people paid tributes to

Bingo, and someone mentioned about Bingo's involvement in the lesbian community.

After the service in the reception hall, Bernice blurted out, "I didn't know Bingo was a *leb-be-yun*. Did you know that, Nona?"

Huh? Trying to figure out what Bernice meant, I didn't reply. She repeated the question loudly enough for the people standing next to us to hear. Then it dawned on me what Bernice was saying: *leb-be-yun* instead of lesbian!

Feeling uneasy for everyone around us, I replied softly, "Yes, I knew."

Although this incident was awkward, knowing Bingo, she would have chuckled and even laughed at the humor of it all. She also would have laughed at the fact that Bernice had embarrassed me with her boldness by pushing *Chopstick Childhood* at the memorial, cajoling people to buy a copy. When I told her to stop, she blushed, smiled, and said coyly, "Bingo would have wanted it that way!" To my amazement, I felt consoled. Bernice was right.

Unpredictable and different, that was Bernice Wong, an unforgettable gal, full of surprises!

May Bernice and Bingo, our dear, departed friends, rest in peace. They are truly missed.

21

THE LAST GIRL

strolling hand in hand
pretending to be sisters
in their hearts, they are

Dolly Tom (Jang), a shy little girl of six, lived at the Ming Quong Home in Los Gatos. I, a shy teenager at thirteen, lived at the Oakland Home. In the summer of 1946, the two of us were paired together in a unique bonding that became a memorable part of my life.

During summer vacation, the older MQ girls returned from Oakland to the Los Gatos Home to work in order to earn money for our yearly allowance. The younger girls were always happy and excited to see us. Some jumped for joy, while others kept their distance in awe of our status.

That particular summer, Miss Higgins, the administrator for both the Homes, had a different plan for us.

Each older girl would choose a younger, Nursery girl and be a big sister to her.

That suggestion piqued my interest. Picking a little girl and then acting as a big sister to her would be enjoyable. I chose Dolly, and Amy, my Oakland roommate, joined us. Almost every day after work and on the weekends, we were by Dolly's side, playing and watching over her. One of her favorite pastimes was hitching a ride with one of us on Edna's bicycle, as she was too small to ride this "grown-up" bike. So back and forth we went, sailing down the long driveway, screeching with laughter, and ending up circling the lone almond tree again and again. Dolly never tired of this, but I did and happily relinquished the bike to Amy. Yea, it was her turn! I needed a break!

Some days we played house, jumped rope, climbed trees, and tried to teach her to play jacks and shoot marbles. Amy had a camera. We took a lot of pictures of us, some on the bike; others sentimental poses looking mellow and holding hands. A few were adventurous pictures of us climbing our favorite trees.

It was fun. Dolly was the perfect little sister—an adorable doll, true to her name.

While I have fond memories, Dolly has only vague recollections of that summer. Her comment: "I remember looking forward to you coming every year." That was it!

Dolly came from a large family of seven brothers and two sisters. She was the second youngest. Her mother died when Dolly was two-and-a-half years old. At such a tender age, the siblings were separated and lived with family members and friends.

However, Dolly's situation was different. "No one could take me," she recalled. "My father had Social Services place me in boarding homes. From 1942 to 1945, I lived in nine different foster homes. The last one in Berkeley was with a Black family. My father wanted me to go back to the first boarding home, which was also with a Black family, but Social Services thought it was best to place me with members of my own race; hence, the Ming Quong referral." Nine different families in three years! What dramatic changes for anyone, let alone a child of five.

At the Home, the girls attended Chinese School, where, as Dolly said, "We learned the Lord's Prayer and John 3:16 in Chinese." Ming Quong also kept the girls' heritage alive with Chinese dinners twice a week. The girls favored this over American food.

All this the teachers did well, but one thing they never discussed was "racial insults." How could missionary teachers broach such a sensitive subject, one that might never surface? Why plant seeds of negativity or create insecurity among the innocent children?

However, racial slurs did happen to Dolly and others in her age group. Dolly said, "There were some mean children who called us 'Chinaman' and teased us by saying, 'Ching-Chong Chinaman sitting on the wall . . .' I can't remember the rest—something about pigtails. We tried to ignore them, but we finally yelled back, 'Sticks and stones can break my bones, but names can never hurt me.'" One positive thing was that the girls always had each other; they were never alone.

When Dolly moved from the Los Gatos Home to the Oakland branch, the adjustments were typical. They involved a change from small-town living to crowded urban life. However, the Oakland Ming Quong had to close in 1958, with too few girls left for the Presbyterian Board of National Missions to continue running the Home. The hardest and the loneliest day of Dolly's life was the last day at Ming Quong.

Only Dolly and two other girls were left. Miss Musgrave drove her and the other girls to their destinations. "I was dropped off at my sister's home in Oakland," she said. "I was sad and crying, and Miss Musgrave's eyes welled with tears.

"I left the Home with eighty dollars that Miss Mus-grave gave me from some left-over funds—or maybe they were even from her! I knew this was not money from my father's monthly payments, as he had no funds, and I had always lived at the Home on charity."

Dolly remembers the loneliness after the Home closed. However, as she said, "Having to leave Ming Quong did make me a little more independent and help me grow up faster."

Shortly after moving in with her sister, Dolly found a live-in house job in Piedmont through another Ming Quong girl who knew of a couple from the Presbyterian Church in Oakland. But the realities of life became evident in this household. Treated as a maid, Dolly had to sleep in the basement, and the husband was "overly friendly." She was not the first MQ girl to experience such a sad episode! "I was naïve," she said. "After all, MQ was a girls' home, and I didn't know anything about the birds and the bees."

Dolly's second house job came while she was a student at San Francisco State. A divorcee named Clare and her two young children accepted Dolly as part of the family. "I was never treated as a maid. I now knew what it was like to have a family. In fact, when I married, Clare acted as 'mother of the bride.'"

Dolly became a medical assistant and worked at Kaiser for fifteen years. She and her husband, Sam, have two sons, two daughters, and twelve grandchildren. "The highlight of my life is watching my children become responsible adults," she says.

One thing that has stayed with her because of living at the Home with so many girls from ages five to seventeen is she never likes to do anything or go *anywhere* alone.

From one foster home to another and finally to the Ming Quong Home, Dolly summed up her experience: "I was fortunate. We were brought up with good morals and good training. I considered Ming Quong my home."

the era ends—yet
bamboo woman's gratitude
lingers forever

CONCLUSION

Decades later, when former Ming Quong girls encounter each other, there is instant camaraderie, a feeling of coming home. That is one of the greatest joys derived from our unique bonding.

Bamboo Women took over a decade to complete, which surprised me. Writing these stories was like an expectant mother giving birth to her baby—but in this situation, also delivering multiple births. Quite an analogy. But each story became instilled in me and became a part of me. As I wrote, I lived and breathed each girl's experience, so much so that this process, with its sad and tragic stories, gradually took a toll on me. I became emotionally drained. Frustration set in, and at times I felt the urge to chuck it all, especially when, throughout the years, many of the girls passed on.

I retreated to my haiku journal, re-read all my little

poems, wrote new ones, and felt refreshed. Haiku was my perfect antidote.

The last draft of each story was exhilarating. When the "final push" came and the correct thoughts were conveyed, the moment was perfect—the birth of a story.

Throughout the entire process of writing *Bamboo Women,* I always felt the spirit of the teachers and the other Ming Quong girls.

In closing, I am filled with gratitude for our shared lives. With love, Nona

ABOUT THE AUTHOR

Nona Mock Wyman was born in Palo Alto, CA. She is the author of *Chopstick Childhood* (in a Town of Silver Spoons), which was originally published in 1997 and received the Women of Distinction Award for Humanitarianism by Soroptimist International of Alamo-Danville.

She lives in Walnut Creek, CA and still works in her store, Ming Quong, with her son. The store, which she and her late husband, Joe, established in 1969, is the oldest extant retail store on Main Street and has been named one of the "Seven Wonders of the East Bay" by the Contra Costa Times.